My Headwinds to Freedom

A Memoir

Ian Cobb

Photo Credit: Tyler Anderson, *The Intelligencer*

Published by Ian Cobb.

Copyright ©2019 by publisher.

No part of this publication may be reproduced without permission of the publisher.

CANADIAN CATALOGUING AND PUBLICATION DATA
Cobb, Ian
   "My Headwinds to Freedom"

ISBN: 978-1-9992588-0-1

Printed in Canada.

The publisher may be contacted at:
Ian Cobb
63 Village Drive
Belleville ON K8P 4K2
Tel: 613-968-9807
Email: cobbiangrant@yahooo.ca

DEDICATION

*I want to dedicate this book
to the only woman I truly loved.
She took a chance on me, and I blew it.
Hopefully, this story will reveal
some of the reasons why.*

"Illiterate, dyslexic, partly deaf since birth,
P.T.S.D. from concussions and abuse".
I discovered the best way to my future,
was to create it, and so I did.

There has never been a book like it
before, I am told by professionals in
the industry. How could there be? I had
nothing to follow, I have never been able
to read a book in my life.

I am super excited and proud of my
accomplishments. Thanks to all, who
encouraged me often, to write my story.

— *Ian Grant Cobb, Author personified*

CHAPTER

1

A Journey Begins

Over the years I have been told by many that I should write a book about my life experiences and adventures. I never thought it was going to be possible. But at seventy-five years old, here we go on Ian Cobb's Trail.

I have been forty percent deaf, dyslexic and basically illiterate all my life. I struggled in and out of school. After falling behind two years in grades five and six, and repeating those grades, I quit school early in my second year of grade seven. I did not know why I could not compete or understand a lot of what was said to get along. I was fifteen at the time, while the other kids in my class were thirteen.

There was no assessment for kid's problems in the 1940's, 50's or 60's. My family was told I was just not applying myself to most tasks, and I was always punished at home and at school. It was the strap at school and the belt at home. I became somewhat rebellious and was in trouble a lot of the time just trying to fit in some place. I just did not know I was partly deaf and no one ever heard the word dyslexia in the 1950's or 60's. I quit school in order to survive.

On the day I quit, I was facing yet another punishment. And I was not going to take it. I stood and grabbed a desk and threw it out the window. The class went deathly quiet. Then I went home, packed a bag and left there too.

Throughout my childhood and for the first twenty years of my life, I was told by many that I was stupid and lazy, and I believed them. Some very sad times. Until the day I realized that my elevator went to the top floor; I was just in a different building than most others.

One of the most exciting and liberating times of my life was when I started to learn to read and write properly at the age of sixty-two on a computer. This happened when my good friend Andrée Quinn moved from Kingston to live upstairs in my home and encouraged me to go onto her computer. I found that the letters did not dance and merge on a computer screen as they do for me on paper, even today. I call it Parkinson's of the eyes.

I hope you enjoy reading my book of how I tried to participate and go down every spoke on the wheel of life that appeared in front of me, to find out if it would fit for me.

I dedicate this book to my ex-wife, Dawn, who to this day has no idea why I was so driven to become successful, at the expense of our relationship. I feared to be old, poor and a failure. Without her help early on, I wonder if I would have made it. It is sad that I ruined our relationship along the way because of my fear and frustrations of not being able to function and comprehend the way most other people do.

We both made a very uninformed and poor decision early on in our relationship. A year prior to our marriage, she had an abortion that left her with an incompetent cervix that we only learned about after many years of miscarriages, stillbirths and burials of two of our three premature babies that did not survive. My first son Jeffrey was born premature as well and kept in an isolette incubator until he grew enough to be able to come home.

My wife had blamed me a few years earlier in Montreal for the loss of her first pregnancy after we married. She said that I was driving too fast on rough roads back from a diving trip on the coast with my dive club with her, and she miscarried in her third trimester. I felt so guilty, as I believed her. We struggled to understand why we were losing so many children for years after we moved to New Brunswick. Until we were informed by her gynecologist about her incompetent cervix before the birth of our daughter Lisa. I spoke to her doctor, and demanded that something had to be done differently with this pregnancy. We had lost so many babies over the past years. And this time he did, by suturing her cervix closed. She had to be lying down in bed at home and in hospital most of her third trimester until they induced labour on New Year's Eve, giving us our daughter on New Year's Day.

I carry the guilt even today of knowing the reason why we could not carry full-term over the years, and of losing so many children, was because of our poor decision in the very early months of our relationship. After our daughter was born, the doctor tied my wife's tubes and we were done having any more children. Two children of our own and a son who we adopted ten months before the arrival of our daughter. My guilt and quiet despair was a contributing factor in our marriage breakdown. I had this recurring dream about the day I died as an older person, and standing outside the pearly gates were four little kids saying, here he comes, the SOB.

I always wanted a loving family with lots of kids, but we messed up big time. I used to pop by the cemetery once in a while. But for whatever reason my wife would never visit. Eventually the love, romance, trust and dreams slowly came to an end and discontent took over. We both just continued on to work hard and give our three children everything we could. I just focused on making a way of life, and I know now that my driven behaviour must have placed undue stress on my wife.

Before you read this book, let me try to make something very clear to you. I am going to write this book as honestly as I remember. I lived a lot of my life full of fabrication, dishonesty and guilt, covering up my illiteracy. But I was always going to make it, no matter who or what was in my way. I was never going to be old and poor. Being young, sad, abused and poor was tough enough when I was younger. It was not going to be the same for me in my old age!

I started to live a more honest and open life the day after Jacques Demers retired and told the world his story. He was illiterate his whole life and nobody knew. He covered up that fact using many imaginative ways. He was a successful coach in the National Hockey League for years. He took the Montreal Canadiens to a Stanley Cup in 1993 and coached the winning Detroit Red Wings for many years. He went on to be a sitting Senator of the Canadian Parliament. The day of his retirement and confession, I said to myself "his story is my story." And never again would I hide and bullshit the fact that I was also uneducated and mostly illiterate. If he could come out and tell the world, then so could I without embarrassment.

I do not have to look over my shoulder any longer, worried about which fabrication was going to come back on me. Thank you Jacques Demers for being an inspiration to me. You helped me remove a huge burden of inferiority, fear and cover-up, and it changed my life.

No one knew anything about learning disabilities or dyslexia when I was younger, seventy-five years ago. I didn't even know that I had a hearing impairment, and certainly didn't realize that I was reading lips to compensate. I did not know that I had dyslexia or that I had headaches and double vision at times from PTSD from childhood abuse and concussions, until I was diagnosed later on in life. I just took shortcuts, and made excuses, instead of telling people that I could not read or write very well. I had no idea why my brain was not processing and retaining all verbal speech very well either. I just faked it and fabricated a response. I would not let people get too close; they might find out. So I just acted the clown thinking that I was inferior. I could recognize many words; however, the longer the sentence, verbal and written, the less I understood the meaning. I sure could not spell. I knew the alphabet, but I just could not string the letters together properly. I knew all my numbers, but I was a disaster in math, reading and most other subjects.

It was much later on in life that I found out that my elevator went to the top floor; I was just in another building. So if anyone wanted to work or do something with me, they had to do it mostly in my building or my way. As you read my book, please keep this in mind. I am only half baked, not totally cooked at all. As I now tell people, I had a lot of red zeros on my report cards as a kid that had very little meaning to me then. But today, I see the zeros strung out on my portfolio, and I like it a lot! Hard work, imagination, perseverance and creativity instead of a formal education were what seemed to finally work for me.

So here we go, with now Sir Knight Of Columbus, Ian Grant Cobb, a story of my life and adventures.

CHAPTER
2
A St. Lambert Childhood

My grandparents and their family.

The photograph you see here is of my grandparents with my mother May in the front, the oldest of four children. In the back row are her brother Rich and sisters Ruth and Flora, the youngest. Rich raised his four sons in Florida. Ruth raised her three boys and a daughter in Vernon, British Columbia, and Flora raised her two daughters in St. Lambert, Quebec and Ottawa. I got to know all of my cousins before they moved away. They were a close church-going family that always stayed in touch with each other, even from great distances.

My dad was also a very good man who lost his mother at a very young age and he was brought up by a stepmom and his father. I do not know much of his former life.

Me with my godparents. I am honoured to be named after their son.

I was born in February of 1944. I was named after Ian Beaton, who was a young Canadian Air Force pilot who was shot down and killed by the Germans a year before I was born, in the Battle of Britain. He is buried beside a small church in Wales. His parents, Doctor Beaton and his wife, were neighbours and friends of my grandparents in Montreal South, Quebec, now part of Longueuil. Ian Beaton was their only child as I remember. Doctor Beaton and his wife became my Godparents in 1944 when I was christened Ian Grant Cobb, with my dad's middle name becoming mine.

I do not remember them but I always knew that I was named after their son, a war hero. And I was always reminded that I was to wear his name proudly. When I moved to Belleville in 1993, I researched and discovered Ian Beaton's military history record in the Archives at the Trenton Air Force Base. Everything was there about him. I photocopied it and brought it home.

My sister, two years older, myself in the middle, my younger brother Graham. Little did this good and loving couple Russell Grant Cobb and May Palmer Cobb know what lay in store for them over the coming years with my arrival.

My very first memories were visits to my mother's parents, my grandparents who lived just down the street from our flat, as they called an apartment back then. They had a huge back yard where all my extended family would gather often. At a very young age, I remember being fascinated there, watching the bees in their large garden collecting pollen, hummingbirds on the flowers, the robins making a living pulling worms out of the lawn, and at times in early morning and towards evening, a few wild rabbits would nibble at the clover growing in the lawn.

My grandparents raised four children, three girls and a boy, my mother being the eldest who lived in St. Lambert while the rest all lived close by in my early years. At one large family gathering in their backyard with my cousins, aunts and uncles, I remember everyone laughing as I ran chasing after the birds on the lawn and in their garden, trying to catch the birds by putting salt on their tails using a salt shaker. I was told that this was the only way to catch a bird: I just had to get some salt on their tails. I spent many hours trying to catch one. I came close a few times but to no avail of course, though it sure seemed to entertain everyone as they all hollered in laughter and encouragement.

My grandfather was a house builder and Mayor of Montreal South in the 1930s or 1940s. Behind his home he had a very large two-story workshop and storage building, filled with tools, lumber and such for his construction business. When we visited, I often spent a good deal of my time hanging around him when he was working in his shop. He always took time to show me and tell me different things. He taught me how to use a few of his tools, hammer, hand saw, hand drill, a wood plane and others. One of the first things that he helped me build was a pair of wood stilts, made with two 2 by 4s and blocks of wood nailed about two feet up to put my feet on. I had great fun walking around my neighborhood on them, making me a lot taller, which was great fun as I was a short kid.

My grandfather also knew I liked birds and animals, and he built my first of many birdhouses with me. I brought it home and nailed it up on the roof edge of our back porch, outside of my bedroom window, using a ladder. Within a week or so I had a pair of swallows starting to build a nest in it. One side of the nest box had a hinge so I could open it and look in. After a while I watched the swallow parents bringing food into the birdhouse to feed their four youngsters.

I thought it would be pretty cool to take the birdhouse and set it on my window sill, where I could observe them more closely. The parents never skipped a beat, bringing food to their young. About three days later I had the bright idea of bringing the birdhouse right into my bedroom and putting it on the shelf that was on the wall just inside my window. I lay in my bed and watched the parents the whole afternoon, until my mother came upstairs into my bedroom. She had a complete fit as she saw one of the swallows fly out my window when she entered my bedroom. She told me I had five minutes to get rid of it, and so I nailed it back onto the edge of the roof. I remember that I had to eat my supper in my bedroom and was put to bed early that night.

About the time the picture with the red wagon was taken, I decided that I would become a city worker and help the workers that I would see around town working with their

This picture is of my sister, Geraldine, and me in my red wagon, that I used nearly every day a few years later once we moved to St. Lambert, as my work vehicle for my first job. I was about six years old at the time. And she was two years older than me.

trucks repairing potholes and such. I used to watch them make their cement in a wheelbarrow and so I decided to go down to the creek that was nearby and dig some of the blue clay and mix it up in my wagon with sand. This was my perfect formula for my cement that I used to repair the cracks in the sidewalks all around the whole neighborhood. I probably filled cracks once a week pulling my wagon and my cement. The city workers saw me do this fairly often and always whistled and gave me the thumbs up.

One day I saw the city workers repairing a huge piece of the sidewalk at the corner of my street; they were about to cover it with a tarp. I asked a worker whom I had seen many times over the years if I could write my name in the fresh concrete. He said no, but he also said that they were leaving soon and whatever happened after they went was not his concern.

I promptly went home to get a stick to use and checked with my mother the three letters that spelled my first name. I did not tell her why, and I proceeded to go back to the corner, lifted the tarp and used the stick to write my name onto the fresh concrete before putting the tarp back. Every time I went back to St. Lambert I would notice it still there, for about fifty years, until they cut out the sidewalk corners to make it wheelchair accessible.

The year after moving to Belleville, Ontario from New Brunswick in 1994, the city put in a new curb in front of my home, and guess what? You're right. This cement curb now bears my last name. If you happen to be driving by, you could check if it is still there. I guess I'll never grow up.

In the 1940's, 50's, and 60's, our family lived in a two-story, semi-detached, four bedroom home, which was one of the many homes built by my grandfather in the city of St. Lambert, located on the South Shore of the St. Lawrence River across from Montreal. Our family would often take the streetcar from St. Lambert across the Victoria train bridge to Montreal. As a young kid I used to kneel on the seat looking out the window as we went across the St. Lawrence River. I have a very large impression burnt into my mind of coming off the bridge and traveling the length of Bridge Street, turning right onto Wellington Street, through the Wellington tunnel, and into town.

One very hot August day our family took the streetcar to go shopping in Montreal. Rounding the corner of Bridge and Wellington streets was part of a poor area called Point St. Charles. I noticed people leaning on pillows and hanging their heads out of their windows of their old brick houses, just trying to catch a bit of air. These houses were built well over two hundred and fifty years ago and were right against the sidewalk that the people's children played on. Some of the people in the area looked so very poor. The children played and sat in their doorways and sidewalks as all the cars and buses whizzed by them on the street only a couple of feet away.

This particular family shopping trip to Montreal was to buy a pair of new school shoes for me. You see, it was my turn to get new shoes starting school in grade one. My folks did not have the money to buy three kids shoes at the same time. Looking out the window of the streetcar in Point St. Charles on Wellington St. I saw a little girl and other kids running around barefoot and skipping rope on the sidewalk. They were all very dirty and seemed to be wearing rags for clothes; there was a little girl who was wearing a dress that was very tattered. She also did not have any shoes on her feet that looked a mess of cuts and dirt from playing on the sidewalk. Here I was going shopping to get a brand new pair of shoes. I was only six years old and starting grade one, but I felt very guilty and sad for her. I know that left a lasting impression on me that motivated me in two ways. First, I was always afraid of becoming old and poor and second, I would always go out of my way to help others who were not as lucky as I was. I still feel and act the same way today, working with charities.

In my early years I spent most of my time in my back yard trapping and banding birds with a converted wire rabbit cage. My dad brought home metal rings of different colours which I used to put on the legs of a variety of birds that were in the area, before releasing them.

I also remember rolling over stones that were around our elm tree garden to investigate. I watched the ants running with their eggs and trying to protect them because of my disturbance. So I decided to make a box, with two sides made with glass. I dug up some of these ant nests and put them into this box home that I had made for them and filled it with sandy soil. I watched for many months as they made their new home and tunnels. Moving one grain of sand and dirt at a time. I fed them and kept them for a very long time.

I once found a young crow on the ground in the neighbourhood, and he was not yet old enough to fly, so I picked him up and kept him in one of my wire rabbit cages that I was given by an older neighbour who used to keep pet rabbits. I kept the cage on my back porch, door closed at night but during the day I kept it mainly open and "Jim" the crow would hop out and onto the wooden railing of our back porch. I would feed him by hand at first with dew worms, liver strips and anything else I could find. I gave him a little water using an eyedropper.

As soon as he would see me coming, he would cock his head looking at me with the most intelligent looking blue eyes for what I might be bringing him. Each time before I fed him, I would blow this plastic whistle and he knew it was time to eat. He started hopping onto my arm and shoulder as I fed him with my fingers. Then I started to take him a short way from the porch in my yard and I nudged him off my arm in the direction of his cage so he would fly the short distance to the porch railing. Soon he started to fly into the elm tree that was in our yard and I would call him for food using the whistle.

Jim the crow started to fly further away into the woods each day, but would still come to the call of my whistle. He eventually stopped coming back in the evening, but would be around most mornings for breakfast. At the end of the summer he disappeared.

The next spring I saw a crow sitting in our elm tree, and I knew it was Jim. He was still wearing the silver coloured metal ring on his leg that I had put on him the year before. I left food at the back of the yard for him and I would use my whistle. I only saw him eating there once. I was sure he was busy raising a family someplace. I kind of hoped he would bring his mate or his kids around someday. All summer I looked for him around the area, but never saw him again.

I don't know where this fascination with birds and animals came from. But I was a solitary and lonely child, and I sought their company.

My father knew that I liked watching birds and nature. He told me that as a boy he had kept a few pigeons. He had Tumblers and Rollers. He told me stories about his Tumblers climbing high on the wing and they would tumble down nearly hitting the ground before gaining their flight again. Each time our family went into Montreal shopping on St Catherine Street, he gave me a bag of bread crumbs and different left over things from around our kitchen to feed the pigeons in the park. I really enjoyed feeding them.

Sometime later my dad read in the newspaper about a poultry show taking place in Montreal, and asked if I would like to go to it. Of course I did, so that Saturday he took my brother and me to it by streetcar, because we did not own a car.

Well, I saw hundreds of pigeons in small cages on long tables. One bird in each cage. A lot of the cages had 1st, 2nd, and 3rd place ribbons attached. There were a lot of different kinds, and colours. The pigeon fancier's names were on each cage and some of the owners were there talking to people about their birds. My dad was bilingual and spoke in French to one of the owners. He happened to live close to St. Lambert. This fancier spoke some English and I asked him if I may come to his place sometime and see his loft. He said "anytime" and he wrote the directions down and gave it to my father.

When we got home I had my father explain how I could find this man's loft which was about five miles away. I phoned this man and he told me that if I came to his place the next Saturday, I could watch his birds come home from that day's race. And after the race he would take me to his racing club where they opened the racing clocks and calculated the time to see who the winner was. From that day on I was hooked on pigeon racing and built my first loft in my backyard. I started with a couple of pairs of Homing Pigeons, a pair of Rollers and a pair of Scotch Fantails.

After a year or so, I only kept the racing homers. I kept homers from the time I was eight years old until I was well into my sixties, when I sold my whole flock to a medical university for research. As a young kid I joined a sixteen senior member racing club. I was one of six junior members. I was just amazed at the pigeons' stamina and drive to return home the same day, sometimes traveling over 500 air miles without stopping. Each week over the spring and summer the distance increased.

I spent much of my time with them, observing them very closely. I learned so many things about their natural instincts. I learned what grains and minerals to feed for best racing condition, and after some years I discovered

IAN COBB

And so began a lifetime fascination with pigeon racing. Intelligencer Photo by Andy Vos.

how to enhance their speed and drive home, using what I observed of their natural instincts.

I also learned from a book I found. I could not read it, but I cut the pictures out and I have them still.

First, pigeons mate for life and the male or cock bird is very protective of his hen and nest box. Before races I would separate the cock birds that were racing on the upcoming weekend for a couple of days from their hens. Then just before taking these cock birds to the racing club, to be basketed and banded for the race, I would let them back into their nesting box area, where the hens were waiting. The pre-mating dance and the happy billing by each pair took place with a lot of cooing and vigor. I would not let the cock tread her.

I would then take my cock birds to the club in a basket that I fixed to my bike. They each received a rubber racing band on their legs. Then they were all trucked in large shipping baskets to the starting point to be released the next day. Sometimes it took a couple days to truck them to the starting point, depending on the distance of the particular race. Races started at about 100 miles and increased each week up to 500 miles. Thousands of pigeons from different clubs were released in early morning together, weather permitting

I raced the hens a little differently. I had noticed that my hens raced home best when setting on ten day eggs in the nest. The hens set on eggs all night and part of the day. The cock bird only set from about 10 am until about 4 pm. When one of the pair was away, the other would set until the mate got home.

I would train my whole flock twice each day. I released my flock together from the loft and they would fly circles about a mile or two out from the loft. I used my Navy Cadet Boson pipe whistle to call them back to the loft to eat. They never landed on anything except for their landing board. When I blew the whistle, they all dropped from the sky to the loft. It did not take them long to land and pile through the bars in their entry doors to eat.

I kept my breeding lines pure by line breeding. I kept my genetic records accurate by recording in school scribblers, using colours and numbers.

I spent hundreds of hours in my loft with my birds. They taught me every bit as much as I ever learned in school. It was the very happiest time of my life. I had one pigeon that was always sitting on my shoulder, and I used to ride my bike with him as well. I built a flat perch for him on my handlebars. I used to take him to school like that and he would fly back home when I went into the school. It was very cool sometimes when I would push him off the bike perch and he would try and catch me. It was funny for some people to see this pigeon turning corners chasing me. Some nights I would slip out of the house and sleep in my pigeon coop. They were surely my first love.

From the book I found on pigeons. I cut out the pictures because I could not read the text.

In the years that I was not living at home, a fantastic older retired British member of the racing club, Charlie Campbell, kept my birds. He was a great friend to me over the years.

What I learned about genetics and animal husbandry from my birds, I applied to producing the finest quality silver fox and mink fur in the world many years later.

I often wonder where I might have ended up today, without having this wonderful learning curve hobby as a young kid. I do know that our prisons are filled with people that have similar learning disabilities as I have.

My back bedroom window looked out over a half mile of a thick wooded area, a golf course fairway beyond that, and a single set of railway tracks that came across the Victoria bridge from Montreal, through St. Lambert, following the south shore of the St. Lawrence River east. This whole area that I saw from my window became my playground for many years, as well as the trains and box cars that were often left on this track. We used to climb on them and walk on the top of them, where there was a two-foot wide walkway in the middle of the roof. We used to walk and jump from one car to the other, just like in the old western movies.

My neighbourhood friends and I also played Robin Hood and more in these woods. We built tree forts and had acorns and slingshot fights from fort to fort using our homemade slingshots.

We made our own bows and arrows from saplings, and we used squished pop bottle caps for the ends of our arrows. I even tried making a whistling warning arrow just like the ones in the movie, but it never worked. My brother and I wore forest green vests and Robin Hood hats that my mother had made for us.

Once, too many of us were in my fort and it broke away from the tree. We all crashed to the ground about twelve feet below. Some of us had cuts, scratches and bruises, while my head hit a rock. I was out cold for a short time, and this was my first concussion. I arrived home a bloody mess and Dad took me to the doctor for stitches. I had headaches for many days later.

We used to walk the train tracks often that ran through the golf course that was on the other side of the small wooded area behind our house. About a mile or two west down the tracks, there was an old round gravel pit full of water, maybe twenty feet deep or so and about fifty yards across. There were some old pieces of cut up telephone poles in a pile that had been left beside this pit and railroad tracks. We lashed and nailed them together to make rafts. We were now pirates. We even made Jolly Roger flags to hoist on poles and we would have raft wars with poles trying to rock each others rafts until somebody would fall overboard into the water. It was great fun.

St. Lambert was an affluent, seventy-five percent Anglophone, bedroom community of Montreal. At the time Montreal was the business and banking capital of Canada. About four blocks up our street from our home was a great recreation area which held a playground, wading pool, youth centre, tennis courts, softball diamond, football field, a quarter mile cinder track and field, and two outdoor hockey rinks.

My folks were hard working, but did not have the cash flow of most of this community. I was very lucky to be brought up in such an amazing town. I saw a lot of quality, but we did not have a lot of the things that our friends had. One of the many sayings my grandfather used to tell me was "if you have never seen quality, you can never hope to attain quality, keep your eyes open and ask lots of questions."

I learned how to swim, snorkel, and dive at the city swimming club, built on the bank of the St. Lawrence

River. We had to either sink or swim there; I remember the very swift current. Fighting that current each day in the summers, I became a very strong swimmer over the years.

I played most sports that the community provided, hockey, softball and football. I was just an average player but no one had a better time than I did. Swimming turned out to be my strength. It was the only sport in which I could hold my own against the bigger and older kids, and I often won swim meets and pool diving competitions.

We were all so lucky to be brought up in such an active community, but school learning was my living hell and nightmare. I was always in trouble at school, I did not know why I could not read or write like other kids. I was bullied. And when the phone calls to my parents came from the school, I was very often beaten from one end of the basement to the other by my father's belt. And that was after I got strapped at school. I was short and stocky in stature and was able to excel at some of the more difficult dives off the one and three meter boards. I remember being the youngest to ever attempt platform diving from the very high fifty or sixty foot tower platform that they had at the Montreal swimming club on St. Helen's Island. The first few times I was scared and I would only jump feet-first. Not that I wanted to, but because I had to. You see, there were people watching as you climbed all the way to the top, and I was not going to suffer the embarrassment by climbing all the way back down those stairs. I already suffered enough embarrassment at school and home. I had to learn how to park my fears.

It was the next year that I made a couple of dives from that high tower, which gave me courage that would prove to be useful years later when I was challenged by an older group of kids (who I had just beaten in a race across the Seaway canal in St. Lambert and back) to jump from the Jacques Cartier Bridge into the Saint Lawrence Seaway, fifty meters below. I said I would do it for $50. I knew none of them had that kind of money with them in those days, and thought that would be the end of the challenge.

Unfortunately, I was wrong. Over the next week they managed to raise the money from whoever was around town and confronted me. Surely I could not back down now! The jump was set for the following Saturday afternoon, and I racked my brain trying to think of a way out, perhaps faking an injury or something. Alas, with no way out, I rode my bike with a couple of other kids the next Saturday on the sidewalk of the Jacques Cartier bridge, over to the middle of the Seaway canal that was below. They gave the $50 to a person I trusted and I knew I had to go through with this brag now. There were a lot of kids who had heard about the jump, and they were on the side of the Seaway canal below. I kept my running shoes on to help protect my feet from the impact when I hit the water feet first. I wore my bathing suit and T shirt tucked in tight, which I thought might help if I happened to smack the water sideways. After checking that there were no ships in either direction, I started to climb over the railing of the bridge and slowly lower myself down until I was hanging by both arms. I nearly bailed a couple times, but I knew I had to go through with it.

It took awhile for my nerves to settle, but I finally mustered up the courage to release the grip of the railing. Instantly, as I cleared the bridge, I felt a strong breeze blowing through from underneath the bridge and it was strong enough to push me as I was falling. I got quite scared to say the least, but I fought hard using my arms and hands as air foils, trying to keep me falling feet first. I knew if I landed any other way, it was going to hurt big time. I hit the water heels first, ankles crossed and with my arms straight over my head. Holy cow, did I ever hit hard. I thought I was going to hit the bottom of the canal as I crashed through the water, I was scared for a moment that I was not going to make it. I was sure that my nose was being ripped from my face and I was very glad that I had taken a huge deep breath of air just before contacting the water, because I needed every bit of that oxygen to swim back up to the surface. I seemed to be alright and swam to the side of the canal. Once on the shore I felt some pain in my ankle. I looked down to discover that half of one sneaker was torn off and I had a limp from my sore ankle, but I could put my weight on it so I knew it was not broken. I also had a bleeding nose that made things look bad to others. I got bleeding noses all the time so I knew I was alright. I was given my $50 as I boasted to everyone how easy and thrilling it was. But underneath this facade I was scared shitless. I considered myself very fortunate, lucky, and oh so stupid; I could have been killed that day. I knew from that moment on, there was never going to be a next time.

The following day two police officers showed up at my home, and in our living room they delivered a severe warning, and did a great job in shaming me in front of my parents. And yes I was grounded yet again.

I had started school like all the other kids, kindergarten and grade school. I was mostly a happy kid as I remember, and I liked school, but I soon was made to feel different from other kids. I was very pigeon-toed and I just could not always hear or understand what I was told. Even when I went out the door, my mother would holler the word "remember" (not to embarrass me in front of other kids) so that I would remember to walk with my toes pointed outwards when I walked.

The very first time in my life that I ate in a restaurant, I went to the Chalet B-B-Q on Sherbrooke Street in Montreal with my mother. This place is still there seventy-five years later. I was about seven or eight years old. I remember it well; it was after I had visited a psychiatrist that my mother took me to. Because I wet my bed all the time, and her rubbing my nose in my sheets did not work.

I was not allowed to sleep over at friends' houses like my brother and sister, because of my bed wetting problem. I was told it was just laziness in not getting up to go to the bathroom during the night. But try as I did, I would wake up wet most mornings. I had to sleep on a rubber sheet under the bed sheet. Each morning I had to have a quick bath and then take my wet pajamas and sheets to the basement and put them in the stationary tub that we had back then for washing clothes with the old ringer washer. Sometimes by the time I made my cereal and ate, I was late for school and would have to stay after class as punishment or even strapped for being late so often. When I arrived home after school my first duty was to wash my sheets and hang them on the line. To try to stop me from bedwetting, my nose and face were sometimes rubbed onto my wet sheets, just like when a puppy was being house trained in those days, by rubbing his nose on the floor or carpet if it happened to wet there. I guess they thought that it would work with me as well.

Once my mother was so upset with me for wetting my bed, she hit me on the side of my head with something very hard, a mop I think, and I saw the Milky Way. I remember the headaches from that lasted a long time. Just another example about parenting of the day. No wonder I was so driven to make it in life. Once I found a way to make a buck, I milked every dollar out of each enterprise that I could. Even at the expense of losing my marriage and family. I am lonely a lot of the time without family now at seventy-five, but I am debt-free, independent and certainly not old and poor.

Another problem that I had was I would have these terrible nose bleeds every time I bumped my nose, had a cold, when I would overheat from running or skating, or even when my nose would just dry out and crack. Sometimes I would simply sneeze and blood would start pouring out. Many a pillow had to be thrown out from blood soaking it overnight in my sleep. It was a terrible thing for me to deal with nearly every day over much of my life. Only when I met an ear, nose and throat specialist after moving to Belleville in 1995 did I finally get relief. My doctor operated and cauterized my nose several times over a two-year period, and the problem stopped. I have never had a nose bleed since. But it had ruined a lot of bedding, shirts and many days for me over my lifetime.

Things went further down hill for me over the next few years. I was falling behind in most subjects at school, and I brought home lots of notes from the teachers, so I would also be disciplined at home.

My sister was two years older and a spoiled little brat who would tell lies and stories about me to my folks, and I always paid a price. She was the biggest troublemaker for me in our home; there was always something wrong with her. Today she continues to be a very sick hypochondriac. To this day I get reports from other family members about her psychological state; she always has something wrong with her and looks for sympathy and attention. After both our parents had passed, she went to my mother's apartment with her daughter and they stole everything. I never got a single item that I was told by my mother and father was supposed to be mine. I do not have any contact with her now.

My younger brother finally finished high school after I took him back to British Columbia with me one summer and he stayed with our aunt and cncle there. Our uncle was a school teacher and talked him into going to high school there. I also took him pipelining with me, and eventually he worked at the stock exchange and money markets. But he over time put so many different drugs up his nose and into his body and became an alcoholic that he had to leave his work. He later joined AA only after destroying many of his brain cells. He still is mean when he is drinking; you know the type. Even growing up he was never a brother to me. I got him out of jail once for one of the fights he started with a stranger on a street in Montreal. He finally got out of his high-pressure industry and started selling worms to sports fishing people for a living. He has since joined Alcoholics Anonymous and I believe he has shut down the drugs as well, I hope. I have tried to build bridges between us but to no avail; his brain is so pickled that he is paranoid. He has bragged to me about all the drugs that he had taken and he thinks he is alright.

Talk about a screwed up dysfunctional group to call family. Including myself.

The school subjects I enjoyed and understood were geography because of maps etc., industrial arts because I could build things and handle different tools and gym. I also liked all the stories read to us by my teachers, including the Bible stories, both New and Old Testament. As a child I had always believed that we would all get to heaven one day, if we lived a good life and kept a direct line open with God. I thank my grandfather for that, because he told me that one day he was going to heaven and he and God would always be looking down after me. I learned to talk to both of them later on in my life. I do not know if they are going to let me in or not after all that I have to answer for on my day of reckoning, but I sure hope I will be forgiven for the way I lived in my earlier years.

I knew even back then that these subjects and stories were not going to take me to law school or get me a career. Most subjects I just did not understand, but I would pick up just enough to bluff, or try to copy other classmates' work and tests to get by. I stopped trying to do homework; it was just too frustrating, and a complete waste of my time. And besides, it took away from my quality time that I enjoyed in my pigeon coop, backyard and the woods. I would cover by lying to my parents and teachers, anything to just get by without punishment for that day. At parent-teacher meetings my folks were told that I was as smart as anyone, but I was just not applying myself, I would not pay attention, and that I was always disturbing the class.

Some classmates would tease and bully me, and this led to fights on the school grounds. Being one of the smaller kids, most fights did not go my way, so I got back at them by other means. Sometimes when they were not with friends and I spotted one of them alone someplace, I took care of business with a piece of wood or something else that would even up things considerably and that they would remember. Attacking from the back worked very well indeed and it was very interesting how they did not bully me as much. Especially after breaking the jaw of one SOB bully that I sucker punched with everything I could muster up in my fist.

But then the police showed up at my door and I was given the belt in the basement again. I never told anyone what he and three others did to me a few days earlier. They held me down and pulled down my pants and this guy poured some kind of liquid on my private area that burned like it was acid or something. I remember running home and jumping in the bathtub and scrubbing. When my parents came home from work I never said a thing because it would end up that I was somehow to blame. Much later this kid and I became friendly and he thanked me for not telling his parents or the cops on him.

I became the kid who would take a dare and do things that most would not, I never lost a bet and I had to muster up and do some stupid things to try to be someone I was not. Or when I just tried to fit in or get attention and be accepted as part of the group.

I could not follow instruction as well as others and I was always put up to the front of class beside the teacher. I could hear better but I was a showoff at times to cover my embarrassment, or just to save face, even though I was very shy and felt inferior. Some kids were not allowed to hang out with me because of my reputation and how often I got into trouble at school. It was a sad time for me knowing I just could not do most of the things kids my age could do in school. I felt I was letting my parents down, who I knew loved me, each time the school would call them. I often felt that there was a large S on my forehead for stupid that people could see.

Lonely and with my self-esteem shot, I remember often crying and feeling sorry for myself out of view of others, to the point of thinking about how I might end my life without it being painful. I thought for sure that I was never going to make anything of myself. After all, I had come from good stock and the family pride was to be maintained. I did not know, nor did anyone else know, that I was partly deaf from childhood ear infections and from the treatment of the day. I had hot oil with iodine poured into my ears, as it was supposed to kill the infection. I remember the pain very well. This treatment probably ate more of my eardrum than the infections did.

I was very worried about my children genetically inheriting my problems. So I would watch for signs of problems. When my oldest son Jeffrey had problems with screaming ear infections, I was on it like a hawk and got him the professional help needed.

In the 1950's no one had ever heard about dyslexia. I only found out that I was dyslexic about forty years later. In 1989 I pressured and fought the school system in New Brunswick to have my adopted son evaluated, because I saw that he was having some of the same problems that I had at his age, and I sure did not want him to fall through the cracks

Robert A. Rubel, M.S., S-LP(C)
Speech-Language Pathologist
Assessments · Therapy · Consultations

• A S S E S S M E N T   R E P O R T •

Name:	Ian Cobb	Counsellor:	Rheal LeBlanc
Address:	RR #3	Assessment:	December 22, 1989/
	Salisbury, N.B.		January 12, 1990
	E0A 3E0		
Phone:	372-5012		

Ian Cobb was assessed for a possible language-learning disability on December 22, 1989 and on January 12, 1990.

He completed Grade 6 in the regular school program before quitting school. He is unilingual English.

He was administered the full diagnostic battery of the Clinical Evaluation of Language Functions (CELF). He had difficulties in the following areas.

Processing Relationships & Ambiguities. This indicates a difficulty in processing and interpreting logico-grammatical and ambiguous sentences. In particular he had difficulty with comparative relationships and familial relationships. The performance decreased as the sentence length increased.

Processing Spoken Paragraphs. This indicates a difficulty in processing and interpreting spoken paragraphs and recalling pertinent information.

Producing Model Sentences. This indicates a difficulty of productive control of sentence structure in a sentence repetition task. The sentence structure on this task is well within his expressive capability. The low score indicates poor auditory recall.

Ian Cobb has difficulty with auditory recall and with processing large amounts of information received auditorily. He can probably be successful in most job situations providing he is given time to process incoming information which he knows he will be unable to recall. He will work best in an environment free from competing auditory stimuli (e.g. others asking him questions as he is working).

In training or classroom situations he would do best to make sketchy notes during the lecture and record the session to fill

107 Highfield Street, Moncton, N.B. E1C 5N6 • (506) 382-2240

COBB, Ian
Assessment Report
Page 2

in the details. He would do best in a situation where he is given a handout of the lecture and be allowed to listen without having to write.

These points have been reviewed with the client.

Robert A. Rubel, M.S., S-LP(C)
Speech-Language Pathologist

Finally, the beginning of a new understanding.

like I did. I went with him for the evaluation and I asked to take the same battery of testing so that I might learn what his problem might be. That's when I found out about my own dyslexia problems and learning disabilities. Even this intelligent speech pathologist knowing that I could not read or understand what was said, just gave me my assessment on paper. I did not understand what he gave me and I filed it away with every other paper that I had in my drawers. I have just recently found that assessment paper and read it for the first time; I still do not know what it fully means. Two pages of his assessment of me are inserted on the previous page. Maybe you can understand it.

I am not sure when in time that I had a visit and talk with my doctor in New Brunswick about my problems with my brain function. I was given a brain scan and a few different tests. I was diagnosed with post traumatic stress disorder, PTSD. But I never understood what that even meant. I thought that it meant I was just under stress. I did not tell anyone about my headaches et cetera. So I started to smoke some pot again. Weak homegrown pot with an already weak brain was quite the combination. I used it and what worried me about it was the fact that I enjoyed it and laughed a lot when I used it. I only understood more about brain trauma after moving to Ontario and getting involved with brain research at a medical university that purchased my whole loft of homing pigeons.

I had poor hearing as well and I did not find out until many years later that I was partly deaf. I thought everyone heard just like I did. I did not realize that I had learned to read lips to compensate. Today I wear hearing aids, and still struggle to hear properly.

The single biggest part of my education that I received in public school was from one of my teachers who I was lucky enough to have in both grades two and four. She would read books to the class. I certainly did not get anything out of things like workbooks, textbooks and flash cards, etc. That was a sure waste of time for me. But she read all the classic books like Lassie, Rin Tin Tin, Robinson Crusoe and others. I was so fortunate to have her twice in my early school years. I loved when she read to us, and I could hear her well because she sat on the corner of her desk and my desk was always at the front of the class and beside hers. I would close my eyes sometimes and I could visualize the whole setting of the adventures of Huckleberry Finn and Tom Sawyer on rafts going down the Mississippi River.

My very favorite book that she read to us and the book that had the largest impact on my life was the true story of "The Couriers Des Bois" with Pierre Radisson and DesGroisier. All about the fur trade, the Hudson's Bay Company, and where all the trading posts were set up across the country to trade fur with the different native tribes as they travelled the rivers and woods and mapped the country. I liked to follow their trips on maps, learn the different names of tribes and where their different territories were located. I liked to follow the rivers, lakes and cities on maps. Where they had to portage the different bodies of lakes and rivers, and how their routes connected through the wilderness. This book led me to be interested in the geography of North America. I could look at a certain name of a town or a specific lake or river on these maps, and my teacher would tell me the name. I might not be able to spell the names, but I could recognize the name and the locations by the geography on maps. This sure helped me navigate around North America in later years.

This grade teacher seemed to like me and I just adored her. She helped me a lot and somehow I made it into grade five at the very large elementary school the following year; however, I found out very quickly that this school was not going to be a very nice experience for me going forward.

New school, new teachers, new rules and many new kids. I hid my shortcomings from other students and teachers as best I could so as not to be found out that I was half baked in most school settings. My self-esteem and my ability to fit in and to understand what was going on was completely shattered. I started to tell people what they wanted to hear instead of the truth. To cover I would joke or do something stupid trying to keep others off balance so they would not discover my reality. I felt embarrassed and shy trying to just fit in or to be liked. Things got worse and my folks kept me in my room or backyard often trying to get me to understand that I needed to do a lot better, inside and out of the home. When a certain test was coming the next day, I would just not show up at school. I would go down to the river or go someplace to not be seen. My brother and sister told my parents everything that went on with me at school and around the neighbourhood. I found myself in some kind of trouble nearly every day.

Once my mother was called to come to the principal's office for a meeting about me acting up and skipping school. I sat outside the office on a bench while my mother went into the principal, Mr. Brigdon's, office. The door had smoked glass so I could only see shadows of the two of them inside. But I could hear this very mean and loud man's voice from the bench outside. I distinctly remember him telling my mother that I would never do any better in life than to swing on the back of a garbage truck. He was a miserable prick of a man. No one liked this loudmouth principal.

One night my neighbour friend, John Hammond, a few years older than I, and I took some paint and some kind of acid from his father's work bench and we paid this principal's car a visit in his driveway. I also made short work of his windshield by putting a rock through it. I knew better but boy did it feel good for all the strappings I took from him. I always wanted him to know it was me, but I thought better of it and never said a thing until today. I received corporal punishment from this bugger many times. He was the one person in my life who taught me how to hate.

My poor parents wanted to back the school but did not know what to do with me. I was being strapped both at school and beaten with my dad's belt, at times from one end of the basement to the other. Because as they told my folks, I was just not applying myself and lacked discipline. Most folks bought into the school's philosophy in the 1950's, I think.

I had to spend much more time in my back yard where they could keep an eye on me and away from trouble. I would entertain myself in the small wooded area behind my house. I got along with the birds and animals that I started keeping and observing, much better than I did with people.

I trapped different birds and put coloured bands on their legs, which my Dad brought to me from his workplace. I watched insects, birds and animals very intently. How they responded to each other when feeding, breeding, and defending their space and young. I built rabbit cages and my first pigeon loft. I kept budgies in my bedroom, rabbits, crows, ducks, and a lot more in cages in my backyard. Neighbours used to bring me injured birds and animals, and I sewed up their wounds with needle and thread. I used popsicle sticks on broken wings and limbs as splints and nurtured them back to health when I was about ten years old. It was a thrill to release them back into the wild carrying my leg bands. I knew then that I would always be a keeper of animals and birds, and I dreamed of being a farmer some day.

I also spent more time down at the river fishing, snorkeling and wading to the small islands just off shore in the St. Lawrence River. There I handled and banded young seagulls and ducks. I fished for perch and bass and I just did not bother to go to school some days. School seem to be the biggest waste of my time for me and where I only got into trouble. When I would be asked questions, I mostly just told any story or lie that I thought would satisfy. Punishment came often for me. I remember many beatings. I knew it was all my fault because I was such an embarrassment to my parents. I had cuts and bruises on my legs and butt. I would not wear shorts until they were not visible to others.

There were a lot of very sad times for me. It seemed that no matter what I did, I always disappointed everyone. I withdrew and spent a lot of time devising things to do alone.

One thing I liked to do was provide food for birds and animals. I guess I was a bit of a Johnny Appleseed. I would take my newspaper route bag and spend hours collecting acorns, chestnuts, beechnuts, and crab apples. I stored hundreds of pounds of them in boxes, bags and pails underneath our back porch. No matter where I went on my bike or just walking, I would bring some along. I had a small WWI old army trench spade that I used to plant my tree seeds in every piece of woods and forest that I could get to. I have planted many thousands over my whole life, in many different provinces. I sometimes look for them years later if I happen to be in an area where I planted seeds.

Even in 2007, just outside Mississauga, I found an American Chestnut tree that was dropping all her nuts on the ground that autumn. I collected as many as I could and sprouted them in styrofoam coffee cups. I donated all of them to different communities around Ontario and I planted two on my property here in Belleville that are about fourteen feet high now. I donated thirty to the city of Belleville for their parks and waterfront trails. All of that type of chestnut tree was eradicated in parts of eastern Canada by the Dutch elm disease many years ago.

Not only have I always planted food trees for animals and birds in the wild across Canada, I have stocked and released pairs of silver foxes in and around the forests of federal parks in Ontario, Quebec and New Brunswick. Over my life I have harvested a lot of fur and it was my way of giving back to nature. I will tell you more about this later in this book.

Picture in front of our family home in St. Lambert, Quebec, 1952. My grandmother knitted this great Christmas present sweater for me. She knew I loved horses. I remember being so proud of it. I wore it nearly every day.

IAN COBB

CHAPTER

3

First Love and Other Teenage Challenges

When I was about twelve years old, I had a friend named Sandra. We became friends at school, she had a great smile and laugh, and I would go out of my way to get her attention. She seemed to like me and after a while we started to do things together. We ate our lunch together and just hung out around the school. She was a big help for me sometimes doing my homework so I would avoid punishment or having to stay after school at times.

I started walking with her home after school once in a while, even though she lived in the opposite direction from my home. I had her come to my house and I showed her my pigeon loft and all that I did in my backyard. She was genuinely interested and did not ridicule me for having very different interests from the other kids. I would go to her home and sit on her porch with her and talk. We started to go together with other kids to the ten-cent movies that were being held every Friday or Saturday evening at one of the local churches and delivered her back home as per her father's instructions. I don't think he liked me hanging around with his daughter very much, and I never stepped foot inside their home. As Sandra and I talked and got to know each other, I found out that there was some conflict in her home, and she was not having a good time at home either.

I was so very proud that I had a friend to share some of my thoughts with. I was so happy when we walked holding hands at times, always being careful that her folks did not see. Sandi became my first heartthrob, my best and really only friend. She helped me a lot in avoiding trouble in the classroom. She helped me do my homework, she covered for me. I would look at her when I needed an answer in class, and she would nod her head yes or no. I found myself wanting to be with her all the time. We did fun things together and we just talked about stuff.

I had my first kiss from her at Christmas after I gave her a Christmas gift. I do not remember what it was that I gave her, but I will remember that kiss forever. She had the softest and warmest lips in the world. When I would go over to her house, I was never asked in. I had the distinct feeling that both her parents did not like the idea of me hanging around there that much. But it was a grand year for me. I knew she liked me a lot and I knew I was in love for the very first time and I told her that.

I thought about her all day, every day. Sometimes when alone I would just laugh and giggle to myself with such joy and happiness. At night I would fall asleep with a large smile thinking of her.

About a year and a half later Sandi came to me and told me that they were moving away to Tacoma, Washington in two weeks. We were both very sad. When the moving day came, and she was gone, I did not know what I was going to do, I was devastated and felt so empty and alone once again. I never heard from her after that day. But I knew I would find her again someday.

About this time I knew I had to come up with a way to make some money to feed my birds and animals and pay for wood and nails to build cages and improve my pigeon loft. I wanted a bicycle, and a radio for my bedroom to be able to listen to my Montreal Canadiens hockey games. I also wanted to buy a real fishing rod; I was only using line wrapped around a stick, but I used to catch a lot of perch and bass which I brought home with pride and cleaned for family dinner.

I also learned to build a stone fenced channel for pike to swim up as they came in the smaller rivers to spawn. This stone fence guided the pike closer to shore and shallower water where I could reach into the water and grab them and throw them onto the shore. My hands were cut a lot from their very sharp fins. Some of these fish must have been ten or fifteen pounds. I sold a lot of them to neighbours and even to the local store owners.

I needed money. My folks sure were not going to spring for such things that I wanted, even if they could afford it because of the way I was acting out at the time, not going to school and such, then lying about it. No one seemed to understand me, I didn't even understand myself.

I started to find ways of earning money. I started by making and selling kool aid drinks on the sidewalk and built a stand out of wooden crates. I picked up empty pop bottles and returned them to the stores for a couple cents each. I searched the edges and bushes of the fairways on the golf course, finding lost golf balls and selling them to the golfers. I would caddy for them as well. I shoveled snow for people in the neighbourhood, mowed their lawns with my dad's old push mower, I had a newspaper route. On Saturdays I would work helping our milkman deliver milk, butter and eggs to customers; he brought his horse drawn milk wagon across the Victoria bridge from the dairy in Montreal to his customers in St. Lambert. I would go to the doors and get the empty milk bottles that had notes of what the customer wanted, the money or milk tickets that were always stuck to the bottom inside the bottle that I had to get out. The milkman's name was Mr. Roy and he would load each customer's order in a wire carrying basket with a handle and I would bring it to the door. Heavy at times, I remember. My other duty was to feed oats to the horse from a swinging container that was kept under the wagon. There were also two different places in town that had horse troughs, where we watered the horse.

Sometimes farmers would bring their produce to town to sell door-to-door and I would help them sell everything from strawberries in the spring, corn in summer, and apples in the fall. After all I already had an in when it came to selling at the door; most knew me from delivering milk to them. I was paid by how many baskets I sold, so I worked hard. I did have a bit of trouble making correct change sometimes, so I would just round off the price to the nearest dollar and I came out ahead a few more cents to boot.

Over the years I often brought other kids home to see my birds and show them the woods and where I hung out. Just trying to make friends. One fellow, Jim, who had been in my class in grade six, used to come over from time to time. I found out a little later that he would steal from stores, and one time he took my brother with him and they stole money from milk bottles at people's doors. Jim, also with my brother, once broke into a neighbour's stand-alone garage and took a BB gun. From the woods he fired it, breaking another neighbour's picture window. They got caught by the police. That is when we found out Jim's extensive young offender's record from the police. Some time later, two schoolmates told me that Jim was bragging to a few kids about getting into our home basement and listening to our family's conversations upstairs. I'm not sure why I did not report this; maybe I thought it was just a story.

We were ten and eleven years old when one day my brother and I came home from school for lunch like we did every day. Our folks both worked and our sandwiches were left in the fridge for us. The front door was always locked but the back door was left open for us. We were sitting at the dining room table eating when we heard a creaking of the hardwood floor upstairs. I motioned to my brother to be quiet, and we heard the noise again. It seemed to be coming from my parents' bedroom. Could my sister be home from school was my first thought. I discarded that thought for some valid reason that I do not remember.

Now in my parents' bedroom, my father had a small race track starter's pistol that was given to him by his aunt before she died. He kept it on top of the inside door sill of his bedroom closet. We had always been told by my father to never touch it. But being the inquisitive kid that I was, I had taken it down a couple of times. I noticed that the six shells inside of the revolver were just blanks with a pink packing on the end of each shell. I had never fired it, but there was a small box of more shells, and at one point I had taken one out of the box and gone down to the coal furnace in the basement and threw it in on the red hot coals. I heard a small pop and nothing more.

I thought about this small gun as I started creeping up the stairs to investigate. As I rounded the corner of the stairs, I got a quick glimpse of the back of some guy, now in my sister's bedroom. I headed straight for my parents' room and grabbed the starter's gun.

This fella and I came out of both bedrooms at about the same time and I saw that it was Jim right away. In his hand was a container of ice cream that he had taken out of our refrigerator and was eating with a spoon. What the hell are you doing in our house, I said as he went down the stairs. My brother was standing a little back in the living room and he said something which I could not hear. Jim plopped himself down in one of our living room chairs and started to make conversation with my brother as if he owned the place.

I entered the living room and saw this smug crook sitting there. I still had the starter's pistol in my hand that I knew had blanks in it. To teach this bugger a lesson, I put it against his chest and pulled the trigger. He jumped up clutching his chest and yelling. We thought he was fooling around until we saw the blood. He flopped onto our couch and I remember very clearly what by brother did. He rolled Jim onto the floor saying, "You're not getting blood on my mother's new couch" I was now in full panic mode on the phone with the police. In those days the police had station wagons that doubled as the ambulance service. I told them that my brother and I had found a guy in the woods that had fallen from a tree fort and landed on a nail. I hung the phone up and raced upstairs to put the pistol back in my dad's closet.

The police ambulance arrived and took Jim to hospital. Another police car took my brother and me to the police station that doubled as the fire hall in town as well. We both sat at a long table in the back room of the fire hall with a policeman. They did not ask us a lot of questions after we told them about finding this guy in the woods, except for our parents' phone numbers at work. We were told that our folks were on their way to the station. I was dizzy with fear, nearly to the point of blacking out. I thought I had just killed this guy. I was somewhat relieved to hear my mother's heels on the cobblestone floor of the firehall coming to the room where we were. I was hoping that she would arrive first before my dad.

The police had now received a report from the hospital and told my mother that Jim had been shot with birdshot fragments. So these were not blanks at all; they were small bird shot. The falling on a nail story was over and we told the story the way it had happened. I was much more worried about my father's reaction for touching that pistol than I was about the police. Once my dad arrived, he sat there very quiet as he was told the whole story by the officer. Then another officer came into the room. He was the one who drove the police ambulance to the hospital. He had a bag of items that he asked my parents if they could identify. There was some cheap jewelry of my sister's, jewelry belonging to my mother, a gold watch that was not working of my father's, his pocket knife and a few more things. The police officer said that he found all these items in Jim's pockets at the hospital. So now everyone knew what he was doing in our home and if he tried to say we invited him in or any other story, it was not going to fly.

The police told my parents that Jim had been in a lot of trouble around town and that we should stay away from him. My parents reiterated the same to my brother and me.

The police confiscated my father's starter pistol, and knowing how scared we were, all that was said once we were home, was that they were glad that we were not hurt. And that they hoped we had both learned a few lessons.

The only thing that people around town knew and talked about was that Ian had shot a guy. My already tarnished reputation was even more embarrassing to try and live down. I found it more difficult to fit in with some of the other kids. So I just went along doing my own thing. It was really my parents that I felt so badly for. They were very clean-living folks and well thought of in the community, with this kid that was always out of line. I always craved for them to be proud of me. But I was continuously stepping into one pothole after another, mostly of my own making.

A lot of time alone doing things gave me a terrific imagination and a sense of adventure. So I would just go ahead and implement some of my ideas, to find out what would happen. I learned how to do everything in my life that way, rather than trying to understand what people were telling me and certainly never from reading.

CHAPTER

4

A Different Education

One year St. Lambert hosted the British Empire Summer Games, track and field. Even our new Queen Elizabeth and Prince Philip attended. One of the biggest events that I remember was the one-mile race. Two of the favourites to break the four-minute mile were John Landy and Roger Bannister. One from England and the other from Australia. The stands were packed to capacity. I was more interested in making a buck than the events. So I got a job there working for the canteen for the week. Selling hot dogs and pop. Boy did I clean up in commission and tips. I now had enough money to buy a bicycle and I did.

I used to bike everywhere. Often across the Jacques Cartier Bridge to St. Helen's Island for picnics and to swim in the huge swimming pools there. We had no other place to swim now because the building of the St. Lawrence Seaway had taken out our town's swimming area and all the small islands that used to be my playground area in the river.

My mother's cousin Harold was an apple farmer in Hemmingford, Quebec. Our family visited a few times a year, especially at harvest time. He was the first person that I knew who had gone to college. He had gone to McDonald Agriculture College and also to McGill University. I was very impressed by him. The first time on his farm I remember getting into trouble with my cousins, having apple throwing fights using some of the apples that were on the ground.

Uncle Harold came up to me and I knew he was angry, but instead of yelling at me, he explained that every time some of our apples that we threw hit his trees they bruised some of the fruit, which now he was not going to be able to sell, as well as breaking the very small branches that were going to produce the next year's crop.

He explained how he first had to prune his trees, spray them to protect them from insects and all the other work that went into producing the best fruit possible. He showed me a lot starting with how you pick fruit without hurting the tree or the fruit. He showed me how to drive his tractor, and in his barn he showed me his washing, grading and packing machine and how it worked. I had so much respect for him and his quality operation. I think it was the next year I had bought myself my first bicycle and I biked the sixty miles to his farm with my sleeping bag tied on back.

Some days I would bike out to St. Hubert Air Force Base, maybe ten or twelve miles away. Instead of going to school, I would take water and lunch and sit outside of the wire fence a good part of the day and watch the take-offs and landings of the military aircraft, including the famous Saber Jets.

I grew up hearing many stories from family members that had fought in WW1 and WW2, some in the Korean War. Some fought in the Air Force, some in the Army. I listened intently to many tales of how each one of them took different actions to survive in many dangerous situations. One of them gave me his metal army helmet with a dent in it. I was told how this helmet saved his life from a piece of shrapnel which caused the dent. I wore it often while playing in the woods during our slingshot acorn war games. I knew how the world respected our country's war effort and that Canada was a destination for thousands of immigrants, wanting a better life for their families.

I listened to stories of the Great Depression and what people had to do to eat and get by and how men rode the rails in boxcars across Canada trying to find work to feed their families.

One day I decided to join the Navy Sea Cadets at HMCS Donnacona on Drummond St. in Montreal. I learned a lot more than going to school ever taught me. Discipline and self-reliance, working together as a group and all about our active Navy, the seven seas, sailing, and shooting rifles at the shooting range and a lot more. I remember being so proud to wear my uniform, I would spit and polish my boots so that they would shine in the sunlight as I walked. I ironed my uniform and used white shoe polish on the top of my port and starboard navy cap. I was one of the smaller cadets but I kept up at most things. I loved to march in parades around the Montreal area. I was a very good shot on the rifle range. And when we played capture the flag at a military base near Montreal my team always won the day. I used to walk with pride, showing off my uniform, instead of taking the bus, the whole length of St. Catherine St. a few miles to Papineau St. to catch the south shore bus across the Jacques Cartier Bridge back to St. Lambert.

I learned how to play bugle in the cadet band. My favorite musical instrument is the saxophone, but I never got around to learning how to play it.

Once when a US Navy Ship was in Montreal Harbor, myself and my chum were in uniform and we went into a bar on the way home from cadets with two young US sailors that we met on the street. They were in uniform as well. I still remember one of the US sailor's name, Tom Marty Nails. They bought us a beer. It was the first time that I had a beer in an establishment and I felt very grown up. No one

COMMODORE AND CADETS: Commodore Paul Earl, senior naval officer, Montreal district, took the salute at a marchpast of 240 Royal Canadian Sea Cadets and Navy League Cadets in Verdun yesterday. The parade was staged to mark the end of Navy Week. Above, Commodore Earl explains the significance of the pennant on his limousine to Cadets Robert Snow, left, and Ian Cobb.

(Gazette Photo Service)

My time as a Navy Cadet. I learned more doing this than I ever did in school.

IAN COBB

questioned us because we were in uniform I suppose. I think I was about fourteen years old.

I learned how to be a very strong swimmer at the YMCA and I learned about scuba diving and hard hat diving.

In cadets I was lucky enough to be selected to go by train to cadet camp at HMCS Acadia in Cape Breton, Nova Scotia, paid for by the Navy. We went by train and I remember watching all night long from my lower bunk bed window as we followed the St. Lawrence River east. It was my first trip out of Montreal, and it was a fantastic two weeks at this great cadet camp. One highlight was I was the coxswain of a crew sailing a whaler sailboat. I had some experience hanging around the Longueil boating club and sailing with other members in the St. Lawrence River many times during the summer. My crew and I never lost a race across Sydney Harbour and back each day. I had a great crew and we came back home to HMCS Donnacona in Montreal with the winners trophy. I remember thinking then, that when I became seventeen and of age to join the Navy, I was going to sign up.

In 1959 the St. Lawrence Seaway opened. St. Lambert locks are the first locks in the seaway system. The Victoria Bridge is the first lift bridge. I remember putting my Navy Cadet uniform on the day of the opening. I had a small camera with me. Using my uniform to get past security and knowing my way around that area, I walked onto the bridge and onto the part of the bridge that lifted up over the canal. The bridge siren sounded and the bridge went up, as Queen Elizabeth's ship, The Britannia, sailed underneath me. Standing on the Britannia's quarter deck was Her Majesty, Prince Philip and Dwight Eisenhower. As I took a couple of pictures Prince Philip gave me a wave, and I saluted him. The President and Queen just looked up at me.

Once the ship was in the lock and the bridge lowered I walked off into the waiting hands of the RCMP, who gave me a scolding. As they were scolding me I decided to salute them and held it until the RCMP officer returned my salute. That move got me out of a jam, I think, and they let me walk home.

Back in school I found myself put up into grade seven somehow, two years older than my classmates due to my repeated years in grades five and six, and I felt pretty stupid and inferior. I knew most of the kids that had left me behind and were now in the brand new high school, including my sister and younger brother. They had all passed me by. Each day and night I tried to figure how to just quit school, but where would I go? What would I do? One morning the teacher told me I had to go down to the principal's office in front of the whole class, I knew what that meant, another strapping, for not doing my homework and playing hooky from school the day before. I stood up beside my desk and thought long and hard at what I was about to do; there was no turning back once I made my decision. I finally answered, after he gave his command the second time. I said to him in a very assertive manner, not today teach! as I picked up my desk, ink well bottle and all, and pushed it out the window that I sat beside. It landed on the asphalt schoolyard two floors below. The class went silent as I walked past the teacher to the coatroom, grabbed my jacket and headed down the stairs, out the door and home. I did a lot of thinking on the way home.

Both of my parents were at work and I did not want to face them with what I had done. My mother was the softer one for me to speak to. So when I got home I called her at work. I point blank told her that I had quit school today and I would find a job and start paying room and board as my father had always told me I'd have to if I ever quit school.

I left it up to my mother to break the news to my dad when he arrived home from work. I was fully expecting a licking but instead that evening was surprisingly calm, considering what I had just done. The police had just been at our house a couple weeks or so earlier because of my jump off the Jacques Cartier Bridge into the Seaway canal.

Each day after quitting school, I walked miles knocking on doors asking for work; most times I was given an application form that I just could not fill out properly. I tried selling myself verbally. I looked like a million bucks in my shirt, tie and a sports jacket, but I knew I needed more than a neat appearance to get a job.

My mother worked in the audit office at the Sears downtown store in Montreal and my Dad was a welder and foreman for GSW in St. Henri, Montreal. My mother landed an interview for me, at the Sears dress workshop and alterations department as an office boy.

I was very proud to have my first job and to walk to the train station with all the other people going to their jobs in Montreal, wearing my shirt and tie to work each day. I was always on time arriving. Some of my duties were to collect all the purchased garments that needed alterations from the ladies' and men's departments on different floors in the store. The fitters had pinned and marked to size and measurement. I brought them up to the alteration department twice a day. Where we had about seven or eight ladies and two men tailors who performed the work. They all had their own work place with each having a sewing machine. All of them worked by piece work and were paid so much for each type of alteration. My job was to record in a large ledger how much time that was allocated for each different alteration and keep a tally of time for each sewer as their bonus money on their paychecks. I had a lot of help with this task from two of the ladies who would help me use the adding machine and keep the ledger.

Things went well for about six or seven weeks. But things started to take a turn. I was making too many mistakes with the books and one lady actually started to cry when again she did not get all her expected bonus on her two-week paycheck. I knew it was just a matter of time before I got fired and embarrassed my mother, who everyone knew and liked in the store, So I decided I had better quit my job rather than wait for the day they would fire me. I told my boss and my parents that I was going to trade school that was sponsored by the trade unions and the government. It was located on Parthenais St. in Montreal at the foot of the Jacques Cartier Bridge.

I had checked out going to this trade school previously and was told that I could take the new carpenter apprentice course that was starting in a few weeks. I was able to collect unemployment insurance right at this government school, as long as each student kept proper attendance.

Inside this very large factory building, all the different trades were represented and we built complete houses inside this facility. Balloon frame, meaning 2x4s and slow burning frame, meaning solid 2 inch thick X 2 feet wide solid planking. We built them from the concrete forms for the foundation, all the way up to the roof and shingles, and then we had to take them all down as well. I loved it. I learned a lot and I was good at it, so I thought. But then again at the end of the course there was a written final exam I had to pass to get my apprentice ticket. So I just did not show up for it. Again letting my parents down. I tried to get work as a carpenter's helper, but I needed that damn apprentice ticket I left behind.

I went to Montreal and found enough work to keep me going. I got a day's pay here and there at different stores and shops. I swept the floor and picked up all the chairs at the French Casino strip club on St. Lawrence Main once it closed at about three o'clock each morning. Very interesting place for such a shy fellow at that time, but I sure had a good look around. One great thrill of my life working around there at that time was being asked by one of the performers backstage, her name I remember was Lynn, to help her reattach one of her pasties for her that had come off. Unlike today, the ladies wore nipple pasties to cover. I thought I handled that job like a pro.

I found a few jobs to do at the farmers' Bonsecour and Atwater markets. I washed windows, doors and floors at shops and stores on St. Catherine Street.

I washed dishes for my supper each night at an upscale restaurant where I met Danny Gallivan. Danny set me up with a fellow at the Montreal Forum who gave me some different chores to do. I played ball hockey with a few little kids while their fathers practiced on the ice. I also picked up the towels on the bench and in the dressing rooms and put them into the old wringer washing machine. I saw a lot of professionalism around the Forum. I ran the odd errand for some players. Bernie Geoffrion always parked his big blue station wagon across the street, and I would start it up for him after a game, to be warm for him and his wife. In those days all the car keys were left in the car parked on the lot.

I often slept on the park benches across from the Forum and kept myself clean in the underground washrooms in the park. I learned all about street predation early.

When the Forum was informed that I was sleeping in the park, I was asked to go to the general manager's office; his name was Frank Selke. He instructed me to meet up with Danny Gallivan at a certain time. Danny had set me up at the YMCA with a room and I was required to report for corporate classes at Molson Brewery once a week as part of the deal. I didn't even know at that time what the word corporate meant. That's all I needed, another classroom, but I showed up because I liked my warm bed at the Y. And lucky for me that I did. There was no blackboard stuff. Just motivational speakers, explaining marketing, sales, promotion, perseverance, advertising and how one should conduct oneself professionally while representing a company and its products. Unbeknown to me at the time I received a fantastic education.

Staying at the Y, I joined the swim team under coach Mr. Ross and also learned a lot from Butch Dechain about scuba diving. The YMCA was connected to Sir George Williams University and I could walk right into their library on the second floor from the YMCA. I liked the tranquility in there as students studied and read in the library. I must have looked at hundreds of books over that time frame. I could not read them, but I loved looking at the pictures and maps.

Another job I did and enjoyed was picking up orders of supplies around Montreal and delivering them to ocean-going and seaway-going ships in the Montreal harbour and the Seaway for a ship chandler. We picked up all kinds of provisions, equipment and supplies all over the city and delivered them to ships from many different countries in the harbour, seaway locks and all the way to Quebec City. All were ordered by the captain, chief engineer and the steward on board for their upcoming voyage. I learned a lot being on so many different foreign ships. Watching so many different kinds of cargo being hoisted or poured into their ship's hull was fascinating to me. I spoke to a lot of different crew members about their countries, at least the ones that could speak a little English. I also had many opportunities to sample different foods from around the world prepared in the galleys on these foreign ships.

I also worked shoveling grain onto conveyor belts inside the grain elevators that fed the hulls of ships waiting in harbour. The dust was incredible and we had to have our T-shirts up over our noses and mouths. I took all kinds of small daily jobs around town to earn a buck or two.

Many months later I went back to my parents' home in St Lambert and I stayed, with the understanding that

I get a regular job and pay board or go to school. I was old enough to get my motorcycle licence at 16 years old, as I remember the test was given to me orally, and I purchased a 125 cc Francis Barnett bike. Dave Sheltus, and another friend Louis La Roche were very mechanically inclined, unlike myself at the time. We all had motorcycles and had a lot of fun with them. Plus It was great transportation for me.

I was working at different jobs around Montreal at the time and all friends my age had passed me by in school and were attending the large new Chambly County High School, in St.Lambert. One day I went to this High school and thought I might be able to talk my way into this school. So I called for an appointment with the Principal, to see if I could attend there. Maybe take shop or something.

He informed me that this was not how the system worked and I could not go to school there. I had not even graduated elementary school. It had taken a lot of courage for me to go to this meeting with the principal, and of course I felt embarrassed and more real rejection again. Even my older sister and younger brother were attending this high school. But I was not permitted to attend. I was very disappointed in not even being allowed to take shop, where I might learn something. I did get a job in the far east end of Montreal in a large printing factory. I had to take three different buses to work each morning that took about an hour and a half each way. My job was to sweep floors and shake huge piles of printed cardboard and paper shortly after printing so they would dry and not stick together. It took two of us lifting and shaking handfuls of 4ft. x 8ft. cardboard sheets and re-piling it on another skid to be put back into the printing press for the second, third and sometimes fourth colour. Each pile was about five feet high. Most of it was for making the cigarette boxes for all the different Rothmans cigarette packages.

This plant was very large with about fifteen lithography printing presses. Most were single colour presses, but they had a few two-colour and one four-colour press, which could print 6000 sheets an hour. There was also a plate making department, bindery, perforating, creasing, boxing machinery and shipping departments.

When we were not shaking to air printed stock, we were sweeping the cement floor, washing up the press when they changed colour ink, using bare hands and rags soaked in very strong chemicals that would peel the skin right off of our hands. We also helped and ran for supplies and needs of the pressmen and feeders. My objective was to be a feeder and eventually become a pressman. I realized others with less seniority were getting ahead of me working on the presses. So I went to the foreman and asked why. He point blank told me that I was not French and that this was a French shop. He said, all you English think you own everything. I was totally shocked. It was the first time that I had personally experienced bare faced bigotry and he was not shy about it one bit.

I was working six days a week, forty-four hours at seventy-five cents an hour.

After bus transportation tickets and board at home, there was not much left for sure. Now knowing I was never going to get ahead at this place, I decided to pick up my pay and leave.

I was now seventeen and old enough to join the Canadian Navy and become a Navy Frogman. I was very comfortable in and around water and I liked the idea of living on a ship. I had been on a lot of them in the Montreal harbour working for the ship chandler company. So off I went to the Navy recruiter's office to join up. I had no idea that I had to pass an aptitude exam. Not being able to read and write the test well enough to understand the questions, I knew I was in trouble. But I soon realized that the test was all true and false answers. I promptly picked one side of the test and ticked off all the boxes on one side of the test paper. Well needless to say, that did not work out very well for me. My Navy dream was over.

Next I tried to get a job with the post office. The first interviewer would only speak to me in French. He would not respond to me in English at all, until he said in English that I could not speak French well enough to work for the post office, and to not bother to apply again.

I found many different jobs, some seasonal and some part time. Just enough to get by.

Early in 1963, without much of a formal education and not being able to speak very much French, I thought I could do better for myself in English Western Canada. So I made plans to hitchhike out west. I had a road map of our whole country. I was going to head towards Vernon, British Columbia on the Trans-Canada Highway, where my mother's sister Ruth, Uncle Stan and my four cousins lived. I had heard a lot about B.C. from my grandmother who often travelled visiting her four children and families.

CHAPTER

5

Go West Young Man

There were two fellows that I had met and only known for a brief time, Buddy and Roger. I told them what I was going to do and I asked if they were interested in coming along. They liked the idea and agreed. Two days later we started hitchhiking to Ottawa, each of us carrying a small sports bag with clothes and some food, mostly canned tuna, canned beans, bread, water, a can opener, a Swiss army knife and very little money. It was slow going; it took all day just to hitchhike to the outskirts of Ottawa. Not many people would pick up three fellows and I wondered if maybe we should split up and meet up at different places on route as we went. We found ourselves on the side of the highway with dark approaching and it began to rain. I noticed that we were across the highway from the freight yard and I suggested we jump into one of the empty boxcars that were sitting on the tracks to keep dry for the night. With no engine or caboose hooked on, I knew they were not going to move for some time.

We crossed the highway and a few sets of tracks. We found an empty boxcar that we could slide the door open and helped each other up and in. From my days playing on railroad cars at home I remembered how engines hooked on at times with a large force. So we looked inside the boxcar we were in for something to block the door from slamming shut and locking us inside. We could not find anything inside the car and I hopped out to look for something strong enough to do the job. After a short time I picked up a railroad spike lying on the ground. It worked great wedged in the door track leaving the door cracked open a couple inches.

Inside the car it was getting dark fast and we lay down to try and sleep using our sports bags for pillows. It rained hard that night but we were dry. We must have been tired from the long day on the highway because we were all asleep in no time.

Sometime in the middle of the night, I heard the box car door opening. I thought it was one of the other guys going to have a leak outside. But that was not the case. A railway worker with a lantern who was checking on the boxcars must have noticed that our door was opened slightly and he looked in. He asked us what we were doing in there and where were we going. We told him we were headed west hitchhiking on the highway and got caught in the rain last night. He was very nice and most helpful. He told us that the train two tracks over was leaving west in an hour or so, but that you did not hear it from him if someone spotted us. He also told us that there were three engines hooked to this train, and if we did not touch anything, we might want to keep warmer in the cab of the third unit. So that is just what we did right away before the sun came up and we might be spotted.

Buddy, Roger and I all sat on the floor in the cab of this third unit, so no one would spot us through the window. It was a nervous time, thinking we were going to be discovered any minute.

After a couple hours it was broad daylight and I heard the train's engine rev up. With a couple of shudders and shunts we started moving. We would not look out the window, for fear of being seen.

Once we cleared the city, we decided that we should eat some of our food that we had stuffed in our bags.

We opened and shared two cans of pork and beans for breakfast and drank a little water. We were set for the day. We found a striped railroader's cap stuffed behind the hanging fire extinguisher. It was very dirty and smelling of diesel oil, I put it on my head and sat in the engineer's chair and looked out the window. Surely anyone seeing us with this hat on would not think twice about us being there. We took turns wearing the hat and sitting in the seat.

Our fear and nervousness faded as we gained confidence riding the rails in style. I knew this was the way to get all the way out to western Canada. We were dry, warm and covering a lot of country.

I had a road map and we followed along on it as we passed by the name signs on train stations. Sometimes we were crawling along and sometimes moving more quickly. Only stopping a couple times, waiting for an oncoming train to pass by.

This trip was becoming exciting, going through the wilderness, seeing the wildlife, crossing the many bridges over hundreds of streams and rivers.

We never knew the exact time of day as we did not have a watch. That was not a problem; we knew the sun got up in the east in the morning, it was overhead around noon and darkness arrived in the evening. Many hours later, we saw the sign for the city of North Bay as we slowly crawled through town, then came to a complete stop.

We had no idea that at North Bay the railroad changed their train crew. The new crew would carry on west.

While we were sitting on the floor of the cab in the third unit, the door opened and this very large engineer yelled at us, What the F... are you guys doing in here, get the hell out of here!

It did not take us long to get off and we ran from the tracks and towards a road that we saw. We thought that the cops would be on the lookout for us, so we hid in a little wooded area between the tracks and the road for a fair bit of time. We could still view the train that we had been kicked off. It was a lot longer than I had thought. We had run in a direction away and towards the back end of the train and we could no longer see the engines that were around a slight bend.

I noticed that in the middle of the train that we had just come off of, there were a couple of flatbed train cars carrying freight and equipment and I thought they would be the easiest way to get back onto the same train, if we were not seen, but they might leave at anytime. We certainly did not want to be stuck around there and for how long, trying to hop on another freight that may or may not come along and stop.

So we made our way back towards these flatbed cars and hopped on one unseen by the crew. This car was carrying a huge steel frame that was spiked and lashed to the deck of the train car with an eight or ten foot wide conveyor belt that went from one end of this train car to the other. One end was a long way up in the air and at the other end of the car it was on the deck. We did not hesitate jumping on and hiding under the conveyor belt, hoping we had not been seen. After what seemed to be an hour, we started to pull out. We stayed hidden under this huge belt until we had cleared most civilization.

It was getting towards dusk when we thought it would be more comfortable if we went to the bottom of the belt, crawled up and laid in it. It was well rounded so no one could see that we were there. I was about halfway up the belt and lying flat on my back looking up at the stars. This part of the trip was just amazing for me; I felt so free. Some of the time sleeping but mostly looking at the different constellations and stars in the clear sky.

That night was the first time since my Sunday school days that I had a talk with my God and my grandfather who had died years earlier. I knew he was sitting with the big fella in heaven, looking down at me. I was sure they both were disappointed with me and were wondering what my next move might be. At a very young age my grandfather seemed to know that I would be doing things differently in life. He told me that not everyone learns the same way, and there were many different ways one gets an education. He also told me that one day he would be in heaven and would be looking out for me. I always knew I had someone to talk to.

As we travelled along, with the wheels squealing, the heavy beams and metal parts of this grader belt frame, that were lashed to the sides of the main frame, clanging from side to side as the train car swayed. I kept my hands in my pockets or folded under my armpits, so as not to get my fingers pinched off by some of this steel in the dark.

During the night going by a large body of water, I saw a spectacular lightning show far out over the water. With chain lightning and bolt lighting hitting the lake miles offshore, it lit up many miles of the lake surface.

Over time this storm got closer to us and it started to rain very hard. We were now lying in a stream of water running down the belt. We had to get back under the belt, but what to do in the dark with this heavy steel moving a few inches from side to side? One of us was sure to have a finger snipped off or worse, trying to maneuver ourselves under the belt in the dark. Slowly and between flashes of lightning strikes that we used for vision, we made it under with no one hurt. It was dry and out of the wind.

In the morning we decided that when our train next stopped, we would find an empty boxcar to get into and out of these cramped quarters.

Hours later the train did stop, and we did not know for how long it was going to be stopped. So Buddy, being the biggest of the three of us, got off and ran ahead checking for an empty boxcar that had a door that would open. We kept his bag. He found one about six cars up and pulled the door open. He motioned to us, and Roger and I headed up the track. Buddy helped us both to get in after we threw the three bags in.

I still had the railroad spike that I found along the tracks in Ottawa in my bag, and we again used it to keep the door from slamming shut on us.

We spent a long time in this boxcar, maybe a day and a half. I never realized how large Ontario was. I remember us sleeping one night and our train shunted back and forth a lot as we slept. In the morning we opened our door of the car and I saw that there was no engine or caboose hooked on. I was not even sure where we were, but we knew that we were not going any further in this boxcar.

We hopped out and soon noticed that we were on the west side of the very large freight yard in Winnipeg and we had to stay out of sight. We made our way to the main west track area, and looked for a train that was heading west. We saw one with engine running and caboose on, so we tried a few car doors but they were closed too tight to open. We had to make a move fast before someone spotted us. It was starting to be a very hot day and Buddy saw a couple of wood slatted cattle cars that were empty. So in we went. With air flow through the slats and a roof on a hot day, this was going to be perfect. There was some straw and a couple inches of dry sawdust and feathers that we just pushed aside with our feet to make a bare spot for us to sit with our backs against the end of the car. After some time we were on our way again. We slowly made our way west.

As we picked up speed we realized that this train car was not for cattle, but had been used to transport chickens to market and the dust was not sawdust; it was chicken droppings. It was not long before we had to pull our T-shirts over our faces to breathe through. The faster across these flat prairies we went, the more difficult it was to breathe in the dust and feathers. It was not long before we knew we had a serious problem. The area of our mouths where we were breathing through our T-shirts was caked thick with this dust. We could only open our eyes for a brief second. Our bodies from top to bottom were a solid grey white cake of dust. We had to find a way to get out of this car somehow.

We talked about if the train slowed down a little we might jump. We huddled together close to the floor trying to make a dead air space so we could breathe. We were starting to cough a lot. We stayed like this for a few hours until the train finally came to a stop. It did not take us very long to get clear of that train car and on the side of the tracks. We took off our shirts and beat ourselves with them trying to get this stuff off. We still looked like ghosts, but at least we could breathe. The train tracks ran beside a road, and I saw a gas station not to far down that road. We looked like hell and we hoped there would be a bathroom sink that we could wash up in a little. Even our hair was matted white.

Upon arriving at the gas station, we saw a sign for a restroom and the door was open. Well, I sure did not want to ever meet up with the owner of that garage. I felt very bad leaving him with such a mess, the floor and all to clean up. I think we were around Portage La Prairie, Manitoba.

After all that time we noticed that the train we just got off of was still stopped on the siding. We knew no one was going to pick us up hitchhiking looking like we did. So we ran back to the train and got into a boxcar. After a while another freight went by us heading east and our train pulled out again. We stayed in this car all the way until the outskirts of Calgary where we jumped off once we slowed down to a crawl. We did not want to be stuck in the large freight yard in Calgary or be caught high in the Rockies cold. We had planned to buy Greyhound bus tickets in Calgary to Vernon.

We staggered our jumping off this train, to make sure of a safe place, not where another track crossed ours or even one of many metal posts and structures alongside of the tracks. I jumped first. No problem. The other two were spread up the track about a half mile or so.

I started walking the side of the track to catch up to the others when someone yelled at me from behind. Oh, oh, I thought as I noticed he was wearing a railroad police uniform and walking towards me. I stopped and as he came up to me he asked angrily, "Are you trying to hop onto that train?" Now knowing that he did not see me just jump off, I said no! I am just walking towards Calgary. Get over there, pointing to the road heading into Calgary. Buddy and Roger were not spotted, but from a distance they now saw me walking on the side of the road and joined me when I caught up to where they were.

We still looked pretty rough and dirty; no one was going to pick us up looking like this. As we walked for a mile or three we saw a fella washing his big rig truck that was parked beside his house. We asked if we could use his hose and we even told him how we got so dirty and that we were going to find the bus depot to go to Vernon. He not only let us clean up, he had to take his truck into the city and pick up a trailer, and would give us a ride into town not far from the bus depot. So we lucked out again.

We bought our tickets and arrived in Vernon the next day. I found out that my Aunt and Uncle's home was up a hill a mile out of town.

They were very surprised to see me and they put us up in this very nice wooden barn they had out back. It had a cement floor in it that was used for a basketball court and indoor ball hockey. I cannot remember what we slept on, an old mattress and couch I think.

We had planned to pick fruit and vegetables on farms in the area. We found a place in town where farmers each morning would pick up people who wanted to go to work. Each day we walked to this farmers pick up area and we went to work. We picked everything as it came into season, strawberries, tomatoes, corn, apples. We always ate some of what we were picking that day. When the farmer brought us back to town, we would always walk to the lake and have a quick swim to clean up before walking back to my aunt and uncle's place. We always brought back some of the produce for them that we had picked that day.

I had told Roger and Buddy that after I had enough money from picking, I was heading south for the fall and winter. I also had it in the back of my mind that I might try to find my friend Sandi. She was supposed to be around the Seattle or Tacoma area. If not I might even try to get a job at Disneyland in California. Buddy wanted to go to Vancouver and Roger was going with him.

When it was time for us to leave Vernon, the other two decided to go south with me and we hitchhiked across the border into the State of Washington at Osoyoos B.C. to try and find a car to buy. They were cheaper in the States. We pooled our money and bought an old Ford Coupe in the U.S. border town of Oroville, Washington. Buddy was the only one of the three of us old enough to have a driver's license. So it was in his name and he did all the driving.

We found a USA road map and headed down US 97 Southwest.

CHAPTER

6

An American Adventure

A fter many miles driving, our car broke down in the middle of the Washington desert. We limped it slowly for a few miles and pushed it into an oasis store and gas station that we were lucky enough to be close to. We bartered with the owner, a very nice fellow I remember. There was not that much traffic at his place in the middle of this desert, and we were there a good part of the day. He fixed our car for us and gave us a tank of gas. In exchange we gave him a few bucks, the car radio, and a very good pair of binoculars and case, that we had found in the trunk after we bought the car.

It ran very well the rest of our trip.

I noticed we were coming into Tacoma. I knew years ago my best friend Sandra had moved someplace around there. We gassed up the car and I just took a chance and looked in a phone booth book for the name Kane, Sandi's last name. I think there were two or three Kanes in the book. We had not been in touch since she left St. Lambert, years earlier. I called the first number in the phone book and I was very surprised and thrilled to find that Sandi actually answered the phone. My heart skipped a couple of beats as we talked for a few minutes and made a plan to meet the next day at a mall parking lot. Buddy and Roger were not impressed that we were going to be held up from continuing our drive that day. We slept again in the car and in the morning we drove to that mall's location and waited but Sandra never showed up. Buddy did not want to be held up from going south any longer. We needed to find work quickly as we were running short of money. So we continued on our way. I always wondered why she did not show up.

It was nearly fifty years later when Sandra spotted me on Facebook. I was just learning how to read and write on a computer and we talked online. She told me that years ago, her mother would not let her go to meet me. She also told me that if she had met me that day, she would have come with me. Her parents had separated and she was not having a good life. She later on had gone to teachers college and had become a special education teacher.

She worked later on for the Washington State Government in the environment sector and was now retired. Sandra was also a cancer survivor that had left her in rough shape medically. She was wearing a colonoscopy bag. But she had beaten the cancer. I flew to Seattle and spent a couple days with her. She wanted me to move out there, but I told her that was not possible and I came back home to Belleville.

We continued to talk online over the following years and she decided that still being a Canadian, she would like to move back to Canada, and also take advantage of our medical system. I told her I would help her set herself up here in Canada. She then drove to Belleville with all her belongings and stayed at my house that I shared with my best friend Andrée, who knew all about my first heartthrob. Andrée and I are not a couple and never will be. But we have a very unique relationship. That I will explain later. After a couple of months Sandi decided she was needed back in Washington by one of her daughters and returned to Tacoma. We continued to talk on the phone and online. All of a sudden things went quiet and I did not hear from her. Until a year later or so. One of Sandi's friends called me, telling me she had suffered a stroke and was now living in an assisted living residence. I now check in on her needs from time to time and she is progressing. She can now talk on the phone a little if given lots of time to get words out. She cannot operate a computer or read.

Now back to our trip south.

We continued to drive nearly to the California border, a place called Gold Beach, Oregon, where we ran out of gas and money.

From the highway we could see by the ocean that a circus carnival was setting up, so we hatched a story together and headed across the field to ask for work. Halfway across the field a fellow yelled, hey you guys want to go to work? And thus was the start of our carnival working adventure.

After the carnival was set up, my job was to operate a ride. Chair swing seats that would circle up in the air. Roger ran the merry-go-round and Buddy had the wooden milk bottle baseball throwing booth.

We slept in our car and in the backs of the carnival trucks, making beds out of the canvas. At the end of each working day, we had to grease and fuel our machines. Then a few of the carnie workers went across this large field on a path towards the highway where there was a Dairy Queen to have a bite to eat or a drink.

Working my ride one day, I had to stop it and tell a large fellow that he was not allowed to hold the next swing chair when the ride was up in the air. I started the ride again and again he hung onto the swing next to his and twisted his chain so he would spin around when he let it go. It was a very dangerous maneuver. So I stopped the ride again and told him to get off of it. He refused and I told him the ride would not go until he left it. He finally left saying to me with slurred speech from his drinking, that he was going to get me. I forgot all about the incident.

Hours after and once I had finished getting my machine ready for the next day, I headed across the small footpath alone in the dark, heading towards the lights of the Dairy Queen. Halfway there someone came up to me from behind and tripped me. I had not heard him. I got to my feet to see in the dim light this big fella from earlier in the day. He was even bigger than I remembered and very much more drunk. His friend stood off to the side and back a way. This big fellow told me that he was going to teach me a lesson. I was scared and worried as I stood up, making sure I was more than arm distance away. I had to find a way out of this and I started to just talk to him a little. All along knowing that this guy had waited many hours to confront me, and he was not there to just talk.

He smelled of chainsaw wood and oil and wore work boots and was very confident that there would be no resistance from me. Standing in front of him and just to check for reaction, I made a quick little move with my left hand and he never flinched at all. I judged at how high I would have to swing my right fist to catch him on the jaw, and I knew I would only have one shot to sucker punch him and run like hell. I coiled my shoulder and timed my punch perfectly with every ounce of force that I could muster. He dropped like a stone and I bolted for the Dairy Queen.

With my heart racing and out of breath from the run, I opened the door of the store and went in. Buddy and Roger were sitting in a booth with two others, so I just went to the counter and sat on a stool. I ordered a milkshake and put a silver dollar on the counter. There was a large mirror on the wall facing me and I could see the front door behind me, which flew open and the big fellow was standing there. I did not turn around but I saw he was soaked in blood down to his navel and his face looked like he had been hit by a train. He yelled at me to come outside, blood spitting out of his mouth. But there was no way I was going out there. He hollered a couple of more times the same thing.

IAN COBB

I finally yelled back to him slightly turning on my stool, just you go and sleep it off. He approached me and no one else in the place said or did anything.

As I saw him behind me in the mirror, I put my shoulders up to protect my head from a side blow. He reached around and grabbed my money off the counter, walked to the door and threw it out into the parking lot and told me to go after it. Still no one made a move to help me. There were people from the carnival, including my boss, a few tourist, travelers from California, I learned later. I prepared myself just like I had seen in a western movie. I first told the waitress to call the cops and I spun myself around, stepped off my stool, unzipped my blue nylon jacket and very assertively hung it on a peg beside the front door.

The big fellow, seeing my approaching moves, opened the door and backed outside into the parking lot. As I went out the door I hollered that he stole my money, loud enough so everyone inside could hear me. When I got outside, I knew that I had to be a Mohammed Ali dancer, because if he connected just once, it was going to hurt. But I knew he was drunk and I was able to stay away from his big work boot kicks and his punches, dancing on my toes and in a boxer's stance.

I knew he was a little leery of me as I tried my very best to look like I knew what I was doing. I heard someone say from inside the store, hey the little guy looks good out there. Little did he know I was pooped and scared to death. This went on much too long until finally a hand grabbed my arm and a voice said, that's enough. I was never so happy to see a uniform in my life, and I told this deputy just that. He put us both in his car and told us he would have to wake the Sheriff up and he was not going to be happy. The Sheriff's office was in the basement of his house and sure enough we disturbed the Sheriff in his home around 11:00 pm as I remember. He listened to both our stories and sent the deputy back to the Dairy Queen to get the story from people there. When he came back he told the Sheriff that one of us was lying and reported that the group of tourists and others at the Dairy Queen confirmed my story.

This fellow apparently had been in trouble before and they charged him. The Sheriff then asked me what I was doing in the States and if I had paperwork to be there. I answered very politely that I was a student traveling around with a friend in our car for part of the summer and we were leaving in a couple days for home in Canada. I told him that we were asked if we wanted a few days work, so we took it for traveling money. That seemed to satisfy the Sheriff. The deputy drove me back to the Dairy Queen.

I knew that we were tearing down the carnival in two days and they were moving to another town. And so we did, after I found a doctor to give me a needle and pull a piece of the big fellow's tooth out of my right knuckle. A red streak of poison was starting to go up my arm already and my hand was swollen twice its size. I needed an antibiotic in a hurry. I had to take pills for a week or so. The scar is still there today.

The next town we set up the carnival again about fifty miles away and I did the same job running the ride. At the end of the fifth or six day, I had just finished greasing my machine when Roger called to me from the back window of a green car that had just pulled up to my ride. He said they were going into town to get some pizza and did I want to come. Buddy was in the car as well along with his friend who had a booth beside his. The guy driving I did not know, but he had just started working at the carnival a few days earlier. He said he had borrowed his girlfriend's car for a few hours to go to town and get pizza. So the five of us headed on the highway to town.

As we were driving I became a little concerned about this guy's driving skills. He went off the pavement twice onto the gravel shoulder with his right tires. We were going down what looked to be the main drag of the town when an orange Corvette convertible cut in front of us and stopped. Two very large football type fellas wearing muscle shirts got out of the Corvette and approached the driver's window. The driver of the orange Corvette asked our driver what the hell he was doing with his sister's car. He opened the front door and told everyone to get out. About one minute later the cops were on the scene and the five of us were taken to the police station.

Next thing I know I am told to remove my belt and my shoelaces and the four of us are put into one of the holding cells. We were then told that we had a date with the judge in the morning. I wondered what happened to our driver. He was nowhere to be seen. I found out later in the courtroom when I was charged with being out after curfew, (I never heard of such a thing) being in a stolen car and get this, contributing to the delinquency of a minor. Our car driver was a minor and was not in this adult courtroom with us to explain. We all pleaded not guilty and explained what had happened.

The judge dismissed all our charges, but we had to agree to be deported, because three of us were Canadians. He called the immigration department to deal with us and we were sent to the Portland Oregon State Penitentiary until the paperwork was done on us. We agreed to leave the USA on a volunteer deportation order for taking work in the States and there would be no charges. A fellow from the Canadian consulate or someplace showed up at the Penitentiary and took Buddy out to sell the car. Also, our boss from the carnival showed up at the Pen. He brought our paychecks with a small bonus for each of us. We now had money to pay for our own supervised flight home.

We were kept in a very large dormitory or room with many bunk beds. We knew enough to stick together and keep our heads down. There were some very creepy guys in there that we stayed away from. The guards use to call us the three Canucks. Mostly they did look out for us a bit. One thing for sure was that I knew I was never going to do anything that might land me into a place like that. Sometimes I think everyone after leaving high school should have to spend a couple days in a place like this.

A week later we were handcuffed, put into a paddy wagon and taken to a room in the Portland, Oregon airport. Once our plane was ready we were put on board ahead of anyone else. We were taken to the very last seats at the back and one of our handcuffs was locked onto a ring in the arm of our seat. Once everyone else was on board, we flew to Seattle international airport. When all the other passengers had disembarked in Seattle, two uniformed guards came on board, hooked the three of us to one of the guards, and walked us off the plane into the largest airport I had ever seen. We walked for about half a mile inside with people staring at us handcuffed together. I was so embarrassed; I thought at the time that someone was sure to recognize me.

They took us down to a floor below the airport. It was huge, like a city under there. They put us in holding cells there, waiting for our plane to take us to Vancouver. I think we were held there for about five hours or so. When again we were handcuffed and after all other passengers were loaded, they seated us again in the back of a TCA plane, Trans Canada Airways in those days, but the handcuffs were removed, thank goodness. We landed in Vancouver where I expected to see the RCMP show up. But not so; the three of us walked out of the Vancouver airport like nothing had ever happened.

We then went to a restaurant and ate something and the three of us talked about what we were going to do now. I told them that I was going back to Vernon to try to find work.

Buddy and Roger, on the other hand, wanted to stay in Vancouver. So we said our goodbyes and I have never seen or heard from them again to this day. I still had a few dollars and I bought a bus ticket to Vernon.

When I arrived in Vernon, I went to my aunt and uncle's home and told them of some of my adventures. My uncle was a high school industrial arts teacher and knew a fellow that had a glass business that made windows and he was looking for a person to train in the glass business. So I started to work for Morgan's Glass. I would cut glass, bevel and sandpaper the edges using a belt sander, drill holes for window knobs, cut screening and install the glass and screens into prefabricated wood frames. I worked only a few weeks before telling Morgan that I was heading back to Montreal. I gave him the fictitious reason of a very sick family member in Montreal. But the real reason was that I was feeling guilty that I had stayed long enough living with my relatives. The whole family was gearing up for their approaching new school year. I just felt that I should leave.

The day I left Vernon for Montreal, Morgan, the owner, told me that when I came back he would have a job for me. I also received a great gift from my Aunt Ruth. She gave me my first young men's winter dress coat. I remember being so proud wearing it on the Greyhound bus trip home to Montreal. I wore and kept that winter coat for about twenty years.

UNITED STATES DEPARTMENT OF JUSTICE
Immigration and Naturalization Service

ORDER TO SHOW CAUSE and NOTICE OF HEARING

In Deportation Proceedings under Section 242 of the Immigration and Nationality Act

UNITED STATES OF AMERICA:

In the Matter of)
)
IAN GRANT COBB)
)
Respondent.)

To: __Ian Grant Cobb__   File No __A-13 491 059__
         (name)
__c/o Clackamas County Jail__
         (address)
__Oregon City, Oregon__

UPON inquiry conducted by the Immigration and Naturalization Service, it is alleged that:

1. You are not a citizen or national of the United States;
2. You are a native of __Canada__
   and a citizen of __Canada__ ;
3. You last entered the United States at __Oroville, Washington,__ on
   or about __August 3, 1963__ ;
          (date)
4. You were admitted as a visitor for two or three days to go to Spokane, Washington;

5. You proceeded to Gold Beach, Oreg. , where you accepted employment with the Hayworth and Nelson Carnival.

AND on the basis of the foregoing allegations, it is charged that you are subject to deportation pursuant to the following provision(s) of law:

Section 241(a)(9) of the Immigration and Nationality Act, in that, after admission as a nonimmigrant under Section 101(a)(15) of said Act, you failed to comply with the conditions of the nonimmigrant status under which you were admitted.

WHEREFORE, YOU ARE ORDERED to appear for hearing before a Special Inquiry Officer of the Immigration and Naturalization Service of the United States Department of Justice at __Clackamas County Jail, Oregon City, Oregon__ on __August 22, 1963,__ at __2:30__ p m, and show cause why you should not be deported from the United States on the charge(s) set forth above.

Dated: __August 20, 1963__

IMMIGRATION AND NATURALIZATION SERVICE

William L. Pattillo, Acting District Director
         (signature and title of issuing officer)
__Portland, Oregon__
         (City and State)

Form I-221
(Rev. 1-1-62)   (over)

I did not have any idea that my parents would receive these papers,
along with my Oregon State Penitentiary release papers in the mail.
My folks gave me all of these papers years later.

CHAPTER

7

Pipelining

I was only back home in Montreal a few weeks when my brother and our friend Jake Carter were saying that they wanted to go west to Vancouver. They both had a few bucks and I had applied and was receiving unemployment insurance. My mother also showed up at the train station the day we were leaving and gave my brother and me a hundred dollars each. We all had our train tickets to Vancouver and left.

As we travelled we talked about getting work in Vancouver and if that did not work out for them, they both would go to the USA and join the US Marine Corps. Although Jake lived in St. Lambert his whole life, he was an American born in Connecticut and had already received his military draft papers. I had already been that route trying to join the Canadian Navy. I knew that was not going to work for me. I remembered that I had a job at Morgan Glass in Vernon to go back to, if I could not find work in Vancouver.

I got to enjoy this trip west in style on the train; we traveled coach meaning we only had our seats to sleep on, but most of the time we could sleep lying down on the whole seat. We played a lot of cards, rode the dome car a lot, met a lot of people and had a great trip across the country. For me the second time and their first.

I spent most of my time looking out at all the vast changing countryside, watching for wildlife and noticing

Ian and Jake looking for work in Vancouver.

the different kind of crops, farms, and the many different ways of life across each province. I just loved it and wondered and dreamed how one day would I be able to work for myself farming and be a productive man. Instead of going from one job to another just getting by.

Once we arrived in Vancouver we found a cheap, rather smelly apartment, advertised in the local paper. Just off Hastings on Boyce St., a very poor and rough area. We started the very next day reading the want ads in the local paper trying to find work. Jake found one that was looking for door salespersons. It was selling MacLean's magazine subscriptions on commission. So the three of us went for a day's training. Each day our boss would take us in his car to different areas of the city. We would work all day, mostly in the Vancouver rain and steady drizzle going from door to door.

In the fall, Vancouver weather was mild but it rained every day and we only had one raincoat. So one of us would work the street houses with the raincoat and the other two would work the apartment buildings. We worked for nearly two weeks. By Friday the second week, the three of us together were paid a grand total of nineteen dollars. Jake told our boss to stick his job where the sun don't shine and quit. Our boss told us what Jake said and he fired us as well.

We went back to our apartment knowing that our next week's rent was due in three days. We decided not to spend the money on rent because it was time to make a move. Both Jake and my brother headed to the States to join the Marines, and I made a phone call to Morgan Glass back in Vernon. He said that I had a job when I got there and they were busy.

The Vernon bus station was right across the street from the Morgan Glass shop and I walked over. Morgan and I talked a bit and I asked if he knew of a cheap room or apartment nearby. He told me about a very big old wooden home not far away that had been made into apartments. So I checked it out. All the apartments on the first and second floor were filled. But the fellow said there was a single one bedroom apartment in the attic. It had a fairly good size kitchen and dining area, sink, small kitchen table, fridge and stove. Bathtub and small sink. An old couch and chair. One good size bedroom, with a bed and old chest of drawers. I cannot remember the rent price but it was reasonable with utilities included. I started work the very next day.

About two weeks after I started work, my brother and Jake, back from the States, showed up in Vernon at my place of work. Both of them were broke and telling me that Jake could not get into the Marines because of his poor eyesight. He did wear very thick coke bottle glasses. Both of them were running short of money in the States so they headed back to Canada.

They moved into my little apartment. The bed was a tight fit for my brother and I and Jake slept on the old couch.

My landlord had verified my employment and gave me two weeks grace for my rent. I had only just received my first two-week paycheck that was promised to my landlord for the first month rent. I just had enough left to buy very little food. I remember the three of us eating oatmeal and hot water for the first week until my aunt and uncle dropped by for a visit. They discovered our plight and gave us stuff from their garden. They also bought us some butter, milk and bread as I remember.

A few days later Jake had his parents send him money, so that he could take the train home to Montreal. My brother, on the other hand, was asked if he would like to move into my aunt and uncle's home and go back to high school which he had not finished. He took them up on their offer and went back to school. I continued to work for Morgan Glass.

I worked at Morgan Glass well into the winter when Morgan started to realize that I could not understand all the written instructions and I had made a few mistakes. Business was slow in the winter and mistakes cost money, he told me, as he handed me my walking papers.

I told my relatives that work was slow and that I had been laid off. I went back to Montreal.

One of the first things I did when back was to check on my homing pigeons that I had given Charlie Campbell to keep for me until the day I had another loft. And I wanted to enjoy Saturday's race with him and the racing club. Charlie had always kept my birds for me. I knew one day I would get them back and I would race them again.

My father got a job for me at General Steel Wares where he was a well-liked foreman. I worked on different assembly lines as a punch press operator. On most of these large punch presses, our hands were harnessed to the machine. As the press descended each time, the lines connecting our hands pulled them away from the punch area. These presses came down with many thousands of pounds of pressure. We were punching out parts for many products such as hot water tanks, pots and pans et cetera. Many of the men working there had fingers and whole hands missing from making mistakes, or even being in the way of a press that sometimes would double trip, catching them off guard. It was a loud and dangerous place to work, but I needed money.

In a different part of the factory, I found out that they had a lithography printing press. They printed on sheets of metal that were made into a variety of products. TV dinner trays, kitchen canister sets, for example, and many others. They only had the one press and it worked the very same way as the presses printing on cardboard. Except when the steel sheets came off of this press, each sheet was stood up on a moving rack and went through an oven to dry. It was taken off at the other end by hand and piled on a skid. But everything else was the same. I was interested in the process and on my own time would go to that department. I asked a few questions and talked to the foreman. I also told him that I had worked in a large printing company before.

He told me that they were going to put on a night shift and would I be interested in learning and being the press feeder for that shift. He asked for me at the personnel office and I received a departmental transfer. I now worked from 4pm to 12pm. And now I needed a car.

So I bought my first used car, a Ford Comet, using a finance company. I gave it a new paint job, Diplomat Blue. I was very happy and for the first time felt somewhat secure and free. I had a job and a car. I bought a canoe that Jake and I used a lot. After buying a 12 gauge shotgun and a 30-06 rifle for hunting, I went hunting and fishing with Claude, a long-time chum from St. Lambert. I often would just walk for miles in the woods alone as well, carrying my gun in case I saw dinner, but mainly I just enjoyed looking at nature as I went along.

I was given my first two-week vacation from work and three of us all from St. Lambert decided to take a trip in my car to Disney in Florida. It was summer and I had never been to Florida. My companions were Dave Hastings, who would pipeline with me later on, and Jim Munson, who today is a sitting Senator in the Canadian Parliament. The three of us stopped at every tourist beach area in every coastal state going down. We had a fun two weeks. When we arrived in St. Petersburg, we stopped in to visit my mother's only brother Rich, Aunt Bev and my four male cousins that I use to play with in my grandfather's backyard years earlier. My cousins took us out to a few party hotspots and beaches in St. Petersburg before we started driving back home to go back to work.

Yes, things were going pretty well for me until GSW decided to not have a night crew in the printing department going forward. And I was offered a job on the assembly punch press line again. Yes, it was a job, but I could not see myself in that poor work environment. So I decided to move on.

A short time later, I was driving my car back home with friends from dancing and listening to music at a club in Beloeil, Quebec. A fierce thunderstorm hit us on the highway going home. My wipers could hardly take the water off my windshield, and suddenly there was a car out of control in front of me. I pulled hard to the right and went off the road, scrapping my car in the field. The three of us were okay except I needed about eight stitches on my chin from contact with my steering wheel.

We had very little to drink at the club, but we had purchased a case of beer for after our ball game we were having the next day. It had not been opened and was on the floor in the back. It was smashed to bits and when the insurance company saw my car at the scrap yard with beer and bottles all over the inside, they refused to cover my car. So now I was walking and with car payments.

A pipeline contractor from Alberta was building a line near St. Jean D'Iberville and was looking for labourers. I went to St. Jean with about six other friends from St. Lambert. The company was Canadian Parkhill from Calgary. We showed up in their yard early morning and we were all hired. I was introduced to one of the high-pressure welders and I was now his helper. This was yellow jacket pipe, about a 20-inch pipe as I remember. As each 60-foot joint of pipe was lifted by side-boom caterpillar tractors and connected to the last joint with a clamp, the welders would weld the first of three welds before removing the clamp. This first weld was called the bead that would secure the thick beveled ends of the pipe. Then this bead crew moved down the line to connect the next joint of pipe and so on. The second welding crew just behind us were called the hot pass crew that filled the rest of the beveled gap. The third welding crew behind the second, called the capping welding crew, laid down a cap weld over the two previous welds.

In good weather and with no equipment breakdowns, we could cover two or three miles per day. Every weld was 100% x-rayed. Even the smallest pinhole meant it was a cut out and done over. All the welders had to pass a weld stress test before being hired on every job that they would go to. They were the best welders in the world and came from all over. My job was to slap a new welding rod in the welder's mitt when he put up his hand for one, never taking off his hood or his eye off the weld. The welder, by tapping his hand on the top of the pipe when welding, indicated whether he needed more heat from the welding machine or less, and I would adjust the dial on the machine accordingly. Everything was done with fantastic proficiency and with professionalism.

I worked on pipelines in nearly every province of Canada and in many U.S. States for different contractors. Pipelines are built just like an assembly line in a factory would. I worked on every crew on the whole pipeline assembly line

I worked on many pipelining jobs throughout Canada and the United States. I observed much proficiency and professionalism, learning many skills from the best in the business. *Photo credits: Enbridge*

IAN COBB

I hired on doing whatever job was available. I was a labourer, I drove truck, bulldozer, backhoes, link belt draggers, chainsaw, and rock driller. I handled explosives, set charge delays, worked with the divers for river crossings, took x-rays with gamma ray uranium camera of the finished welds and developed them, and did a host of more jobs on and off the right of way.

We made a lot of money when we were working seven days a week, but there were many times when we waited for the next job to kick off. I had to budget my dollars knowing I could be out of work for a month or more waiting for the next job to start, and living in hotels and motels.

Over many years there were a lot of guys from St. Lambert who worked pipeline with me: Jake Carter, Wil-John Hennessy, Dave Hastings, my brother Graham, just to name a few.

As I write this book more than fifty-five years later, I am trying to figure out the different job locations and in which years. So I took a chance in phoning two of them yesterday, not knowing if they were still at the phone numbers I had for them in my old address book. Or even if they were still living. Jake had been deceased for some years. But I had great conversations reminiscing with Wil-John and Dave Hastings. They both helped me piece together some of the different time frames and jobs that I had not remembered. They also reminded me of some of the crazy times we all had as well. In the first few years of making great money, there was a lot of beer consumed. But we knew if we were late any morning being in the company yard for work, someone else would be hired and we would be out of work. At six in the morning, there were always men in the yard with their lunch in their hand hoping to get hired on.

One job in Ontario that I remember, there must have been ten or twelve of us. We were all hired onto different crews. We shared hotel rooms, some stayed at campgrounds and various lodging facilities that were available. Sometimes we just had to take what was available because as the pipeline progressed along hundreds of miles each town or area had to lodge hundreds of men. Some of the more senior pipeliners travelled from job to job and lived with their families in their motor homes.

Over time pipeliners from across Canada got to know each other well. You find out very quickly who are the best foreman, best welders, operators, and workers. And most importantly who are the safest men to work with. This pipeline work is very dangerous to be around if you don't know what you are doing. I have seen more than one person injured badly through carelessness.

I showed up in a yard at one job in Ontario and they were looking for men for the ditching crew. Part of the ditching crew was the drilling and powder crew, powder meaning dynamite. When the right of way went through areas of solid rock, the ditching machine and backhoes could not dig the ditch until the rock had been blasted. I had worked a job for a short time, drilling holes and I had loaded holes with sticks of powder. They were looking for a powder foreman with experience. My hand went up immediately and I was hired foreman.

As it turned out, there was a great deal of rock to blast on this job, and one particular spot after the drillers had drilled patterns of five holes in the ditch for about a quarter mile. A pattern of five means one hole at one side of the ditch, another across from it at the other side, then move down the ditch a few feet and drill one in the middle of the ditch and so on. I loaded the holes. At the end of the first stick, using my dynamite tool to make a hole, I inserted my cord, tied it off and dropped it into the hole, and then I added another stick. The end of the cord I cut off, leaving it lying on the top of the ditch.

After doing this for each hole, I laid my main cord the full length in the center of the ditch. Then I attached each hole cord to the main cord. At intervals in the main line, about every forty feet, I would put in a delay, so the blast had a very slight ripple effect. As it turned out in one area that we set powder, the rock was not fractured enough for the backhoes to be able to dig. This cost the company a lot of time and money to re-drill and blast again. I was given shit big time the next morning for not using enough powder, costing the company a lot of money.

A day or two later in the area that we next drilled with this same type of solid rock, the ditch went through a swamp that sat on top of the rock. The drillers had put into the tops of their drilled holes sticks to block mud and stones falling into the three or four feet deep holes. Water in the holes was not a problem for me, as the dynamite sticks were put down each hole. Large boxes of dynamite sticks were staggered along the right away for us. As was everything used to build a pipeline by the stringing crews.

Well, this swamp smelled very badly from rotting matter in the heat of summer and not much fun to work in. After being raked over the coals a couple of days earlier by my boss for not using enough powder, I decided I would use a lot more for each hole here. No one relished the idea of having to go through this swamp again. I was not about to be scolded a second time that might even cost me my job. So instead of loading two sticks per hole I loaded four, and in the center of the five pattern, I loaded five sticks sometimes. I was finding that as I loaded the holes my men had to go further and further up the line to bring more boxes of sticks for me. I sent one of them back to the yard with the half-ton truck to get more for me.

Once everything was loaded and ready to blow, the tractors brought in huge mats to lay over the ditch blast area, like we always did to make sure that rock would not fly onto farmers' fields but stay on the right away. These mats weighed many tons, some made of heavy cables and some made with hundreds of tires lashed by cable together.

After making sure the half-mile area was clear, I hollered "Fire in the Hole" and set off the charge. Well, I wish I had had a camera. Because I do not know if I can do this scene justice to describe it. The mats looked like small matchboxes up in the air, a lot of the rock was thrown many feet off the right away, and there was not a drop of water from the swamp to be found. My crew and I had a bit of a chuckle, but with some fear about what was going to be said to us this time.

I was asked what had happened and I told them. All my boss said was, I sure hope you have things figured out now. He told me to hire every person not working that was in the yard and get them to start picking rocks off the farmers' fields. The rest of that job went very well as I remember.

On one occasion I was between jobs and staying at the Carlton Hotel in Calgary. I was having a couple pints in the beer parlor with two strangers. I happened to tell them that I was out of work at the moment. One of these fellows told me he owned a logging company and would I like to have a job as a choker. I had no idea what a choker was supposed to do. But I was one who would never turn down a job offer, and I needed one. I was sitting the next morning in the front seat of his truck and heading into the foothills of the Rockies, many miles past Canmore, Alberta. We arrived at his logging camp just before dusk and he pointed to a cabin and called an older fellow to come over and meet his new bunkmate, which was me. His name was Tom, and he took me over to the cabin and I put my bag at the end of a bunk that he said was mine.

There were four beds and a small table. The other fellows were not back at camp from the woods yet. The cabin smelled very heavily of chainsaw oil, sawdust and a few unmentionables. I asked Tom a few questions and he showed me around the camp. I asked him what a choker was and he told me that a choker (me) is assigned to a tow cat and operator. My job was to pull a 2-inch cable with an eye on the end, and to wrap it around a couple of trees, now logs because all the limbs had been removed after being felled. And to thread the end of this choker cable through the eye on the other end, making a choke hold on these logs. I then had to pull the very heavy cable over all the brush and limbs on the ground, from the winch on the back of the caterpillar tractor, and hook it to the end of the choker cable. The operator would pull these logs out of the woods to the logging road to be piled.

The first morning, just pulling the choker cable into the bush, I could not believe how heavy it was. I had been given leather gloves, by the way. And I had my work boots, jeans, T-shirt and jean jacket. It was a very warm spring day. The minute I went in the bush the black flies starting eating their dinner, me! And when we started to pull logs out, clouds of them rose up out of the brush. I had never seen or experienced anything like it in my life.

I remembered when hopping the boxcars having to tie my t-shirt around my head to breathe through and I did the same thing. I'm sure some of these flies were big enough to carry ounces of me away at a time. They were in my eyes, ears and nose by the hundreds. I was bleeding from any skin that was uncovered. It sure was not a fun day at the office.

When we got back to camp, I headed for the communal shower to clean up. After I washed the blood and dirt off, I looked at my swollen eyes and bites all over me. All I had was some Noxzema skin cream with me and I covered myself with it. It did relieve some of the pain and I headed for the cabin. Two of my roommates were there and I asked them how it was that the flies did not seem to bother them like me. They had a little fun at my expense, telling me a few tall tales about how the boss would always find young pink-skinned kids to work with the crews so that the flies would eat them and the more productive men on the job would not be bothered very much. I really only had to look at these fellows' faces to see that these guys had skin like leather from years of working in the bush.

One fellow gave me a bottle of some kind of oil repellent to use the next day. It seemed to help some, but the flies were still in my nose, eyes, ears and throat. It was miserable to say the least. After the second day I thought of quitting but went to work for two more days. I was not one to quit very easily. But I had had enough and I went to my boss who brought me to the camp feeling a little embarrassed and I told him that I appreciated the opportunity but this was not for me. He told me that he had seen bums like me before and that I would never amount to anything in life. He also said that he gave me a free ride into his camp and I would have to find my own way out. I told him that I would not take any pay for my five days work if he would let me get a ride with one of his logging trucks out. He told me to F--- off and handed me my check. I gave half of my pay to one of his logging truck drivers who agreed to take me out. When he dropped me off, the driver, a decent fellow, gave my money back to me. I went back to the Carlton Hotel. I never told anyone that I had quit a job.

Once my brother, Jake and I found ourselves out of work in Edmonton, Alberta. We waited a long time for the next job to kick off. Money got very tight in the middle of that winter. We stayed at the Georgia Steam Bathhouse at the corner of Jasper and 96th Ave., a dollar a night flop house. With money running out and summer over, my brother and Jake decided to head back to Montreal and I hunkered down in the flop house.

I used to walk a fair distance for a hot meal that a fellow staying at the flop house told me about at the Salvation

Army. They are very good people. I ate a hot meal there every day for some time and they never asked for a thing. They have been one of my favourite charities to donate to ever since.

A lot of oil and pipeline workers used to stay or visit at the same hotels in every city and would all catch up with information about upcoming contracts and such over a few pints in the beer parlors. I also would go to these hotels for the latest information about upcoming pipeline work and the different contracts. I do not remember the name of the hotel in Edmonton but the hotel everyone stayed in Calgary was the Carlton.

A welder that I had once worked for in Ontario told me that he was just hired out to Pipeline Co. that were kicking off building about a 250-mile piece of a pipeline that stretched about a hundred and twenty-five miles from either side of their newly constructed winter camp. It was located many miles north of Lac la Biche, Alberta, and that town was far north of Fort McMurray. I asked him if he needed a helper and he said no, he had a nephew as his helper ever since the job that we had worked together in Ontario. I asked him if I could catch a ride up to that camp. He told me I could, but I had better have a job before we left. He said it was so isolated in the middle of nowhere and I would have no way out once there if I could not get hired on. He said there was only a hundred miles of a bulldozed road into this camp. He also told me it was close to the North West Territories and I better have good clothing if I was going up there.

I needed the work so I told him I knew a foreman that was working that job and was pretty sure of getting hired, which was just a fabrication. So he picked up his nephew and a couple of days later we left for this camp.

It was a lot longer drive than I originally thought into the camp. After we got to Lac La Biche, we travelled a frozen muskeg road made by bulldozers and at a very slow speed through the bush until we got to the camp. We arrived at the end of the work day and it was already dark. The camp yard had all the machines, trucks, buses, parked and running. Long trailers of small two-bed sleeping quarters were in rows. There were office trailers connected to other trailers used for laundry, and a lounging room for the workers, three very large kitchens and dining hall trailers connected together. Parts and supplies trailers.

The spread boss came out of his office trailer to see who had just arrived and told the welder and his helper to sign in and they would be assigned their quarters. He asked me who I was and was pissed off that I had just shown up to ask for work. But he assigned me to a sleeping area, saying he could not very well turn me away in the middle of the wilderness. I was to report to him after I ate breakfast in the morning. I did and he gave me a job as a night mechanics helper and introduced me to one of the two night master mechanics who went by the name of Frenchy.

Every night the two night mechanics drove their trucks, one going about a hundred and twenty-five miles north from the camp and the other would drive the same distance south. We would drive on the main road and then we got to each shoofly road into the right away, where all the operators parked their equipment running for the night. Our job was to check on every piece of equipment on the whole right away every night to make sure they were all running. We also checked the oil and antifreeze level in each piece of equipment.

It was 50 to 75 degrees Fahrenheit below zero there at night. If anything stopped running for even an hour or two, it would freeze solid and be unable to start. A few times we found a tractor or some other piece of equipment not running. There were various ways we used to get them running for the crews that are bused out to different parts of the 200-mile right away in the morning.

If we found a piece of equipment so cold that it would not start, we used a parachute to drape over the whole machine. Next we used a Herman propane fired heater to blow hot air under the parachute until the oil thinned enough for the engine to start.

This pipeline had to be built in the dead of winter because it ran through many miles of muskeg which only freezes about two feet at the most. We only had a few months to build and finish it before the frozen ground became too wet to get equipment onto. To this day there is equipment all over the north that had broken through the frozen muskeg and sunk. They could never remove them, frozen solid in winter and in summer too wet to get to for salvage. Plus over time in summer they keep sinking further.

Sometimes we worked all day as well if more mechanics were needed on the line somewhere. I remember seeing so many things that I had never heard of before. Such as when the sun came up in the frosty morning, I saw and heard some of the small spruce trees just explode when the sun hit them. They were that frozen. Now I understood why the trees of the far north forest were dwarf. I saw a full five-gallon can of antifreeze left on the side of the right away split wide open from freezing. I always wondered if it had been diluted with some water. I loved seeing the wild animals, deer, elk, moose, wolf, wolverine as well as hearing the calls of the largest ravens I had ever seen. Once, two deer nearly hit me as they ran right by me and into the bush at full speed; not five seconds behind them were four wolves in hot pursuit and not deterred by us one bit as they chased their dinner. I saw a lot of wildlife at times just standing on the right away and it sure made my day. One really neat morning a band of wild horses stepped out of the bush. They looked like ghosts with very long shaggy coats covered in ice and frost. There were about twelve of them and I wondered how in the world they could survive in this harsh climate.

The climate was very clear, cold and the air was super dry. I remember turning my face towards the sun and feeling a little warmth from it, even though it might have been 50 below F. There was very little snow on the ground there; it was just too cold to snow.

It was one of the highlights of the day when we got back to camp and sat down in the dining hall. The food was fantastic, all you could eat. I remember the two-inch thick T-bone steaks very well. Everyone had to make their own lunch in the dining hall the night before to take out to the job site for the next day. We had our choice of so much it was incredible. We could even brown bag the steaks if we wanted.

Another highlight of that job, was one night with Frenchy my mechanic, who I had been working with now for about a month and a half. We found ourselves about eighty miles down the pipeline road on one of the side shooflies when our truck just up and died on us. I think it was just before midnight when that happened. I was not too concerned; after all I was with an old time master mechanic, who I had seen do some phenomenal work on all kinds of heavy machinery. And this was only a one-ton mechanics truck. Well Frenchy was under the hood for a long time, me standing beside him, holding the spotlight and handing him tools. He changed just about everything on the motor, and still it would not start.

We were just far enough away from camp in an area that our truck radio was of no value to us. It would not reach the camp from where we were. We were on our own.

We both were starting to get cold. We both had arctic thermal underwear, very good felt-lined boots and mitts, heavy coveralls, insulated vests and our parkas. But we were starting to get quite cold, especially our feet and hands. We thought that we had better get a fire going but there was not much for wood that we could use. So Frenchy instructed me to empty the truck of all tools and equipment which we laid on the side of the right away, including all our stuff that was in the cab.

On the back of the truck, right behind the cab we had a fuel tank that was divided in half. Half for gas and half for diesel fuel. At about two or three in the morning, Frenchy took his cold chisel and hammer to the bottom of each tank. He drained most of both sides before he soaked a partly used roll of toilet paper in the fuel, lit it and threw it into the back of the truck. It was a very hot fire for a long while. I felt like a hot dog turning around and around for hours the rest of the night. We were worried that one side of us would be to warm and we might start to perspire and then we would freeze. We lifted our boots off the ground until they started to smoke to get some warmth to our toes that we could not feel anymore. So as one part of our bodies was facing the hot fire, the other part of us got very cold, we turned all night.

As the heat from the steel finally abated and the sun started coming up, the first bus showed up with the crew. We were on that bus in a heartbeat and I remember walking to the bus not having any feeling in my feet. They just felt like they were not even there. If the bus had been another couple of hours, I'm sure we would have lost fingers, nose or toes to frostbite. It was very close. The bus was warm and the driver brought us back to camp. I thought we might get fired or something for taking that action and burning our truck. Instead, we were commended for taking the only action that we could to save our lives that night.

After we had been checked out by the camp nurse we headed for our beds and I slept like a baby. When we woke up and by the time we ate our supper after a great sleep, Frenchy told me that we had a new mechanic truck in the yard running and waiting for us. We drove it over to the parts and supplies trailer in the yard to pick up oil, grease and some other supplies including another couple of rolls of toilet paper. We headed back to the burned out wreckage area, loaded up our tools and things and we went to work.

This was about a three-month job and the only thing to do between long hours of work was to sleep, read, which I could not, and play cards in the recreation trailer. Well, I had not played a lot of cards other than fish, and hearts. Never poker, but that is all that was being played there. When working the day shift for a few days, I went to the recreation hall in the evening and was asked to sit down and play cards with about six other fellows. The game was called 21 and a couple fellows told me how to play: 10 for a face card, 11 or 1 for an ace. That seemed to be easy enough for me to understand. I was very slow at figuring out and adding the other cards. The winner was the closest to get to 21. The winner took the pot.

Not to appear too much the simpleton and to try and fit in, I took out of my wallet one of my three or four paychecks. Each one was for two weeks pay. One of the welders cashed it for me and I started to play. It was not very long before that two-week paycheck was gone and I was ridiculed into cashing another. A short time later I decided that working this hard in this environment for my money to let these turkeys take it from me, I left the table.

That night in bed, I remembered why I was working so hard; it was to pay off the finance company that I owed for my car that I scrapped on the highway, and I was now in debt and without wheels. I thought to myself how stupid of me to do this just trying to make friends. So I made a deal and promise with myself, that I would go to the card game again the next night and play only when I had 21 in my hand and I would not take anymore than the $200 out of my pocket. Bluffing was not working for me. If I won or if I lost it, I would never gamble in my life again. As it turned out I won most of what I lost the night before, put it in my pocket and walked off the table. These men were not very happy and one of them took a swing at me. I thought, so these are the friends I was trying to make. NOT! I learned another large lesson and to this day I have never gambled, not even to buy a lotto ticket, ever.

That same night I made another deal with myself, I would take every cent that I made except what I needed for food and lodging and give it to the finance company and also I would never borrow money in my life again. If I wanted another car, I would earn and pay for it cash. I have never borrowed any money since except for taking a small loan from the New Brunswick agricultural adjustment board to buy my first house and farm land in 1975. This was paid off in three years and I have lived my life debt-free other than that one time.

After this camp job, the next one was back in Rouyn Noranda, Quebec. So I bought a train ticket and headed back to St. Lambert and met up with some of my friends that were planning to also go to this job.

I first went to the finance company and gave them all but $100 of the money I had made. I was now a year and a half ahead of my payments. I bought a train ticket to Rouyn Noranda and four of us moved into the hotel there. The next day we all went to the pipeline yard and they told us they would not be kicking off the job there for about another month when the ground dried out more from a very wet spring. After my train ticket and a week at the hotel, I knew it was going to be very tough to make it for a month eating and paying my hotel room for a month without any cash flow. I needed to find a little work around there. So I knocked on the door of nearly every business in the town to no avail. Again I did not speak enough French or have a skill to apply there.

Two weeks later, I found myself with not enough to pay my week's hotel room and I headed to the office of the same finance company that I had just given hundreds of dollars to, a few weeks earlier. I spoke to the manager and told him I only needed $50 to get me through to my first paycheck working on the pipeline that was going to start in a couple of weeks. He told me right then that his company policy was that if you were not working they would not lend any money. I explained my situation to him and that he could phone the manager in St. Lambert, Mr. Archambeau and he would certainly tell him that I was a year and a half ahead on my account payments. And I also gave him the phone number and name of the person that I was going to be working for and he could call him to verify. And I told him again that I had to pay my hotel bill by the next day. He said that he did not care and reiterated his company's policy. If not working, no loan. I then told him as I left, that I would be in his office tomorrow morning for my $50.

The next morning I walked right into his office where he was sitting at his desk. I asked him for the $50 and he refused. I then told him that that was a very poor decision on his part. It had just cost me my job and I would have to hitchhike back to St. Lambert without even having enough money for breakfast. He was unfazed. Before I left I told him that his company would never ever receive a cent from me, even if ordered by a court someday. I walked out and to this day they have never received another cent from me. I never ducked them over the years, and every time they would contact me, I always ask the manager over to my home for a coffee. They always wanted to clean up delinquent accounts. I told them the same story. Some left threatening me and some left saying that it must have been a rookie manager that refused giving me $50. Either way they were out $3000 over fifty years ago.

I managed to catch a ride to Montreal with a truck driver. I met one of my friends, Tom Burns, in St. Lambert who put me up in his apartment until I found work and got back on my feet again.

I got a job working for Savin business machines as a panel truck driver, delivering machines to businesses and servicing machines throughout the city with paper, ink and repairs.

That winter I worked for the city of St. Lambert taking care of one of their many chalets and hockey rinks. I shoveled snow, watered the rink each night and kept the chalet neat and orderly.

In the spring a few of us were hired by Banister Pipeline Co. that was putting in a line from Bowmanville east to Brockville along the north shore of lake Ontario. After that, another job near the Sarnia and London area. When that contract was finished I went with Dave Hastings and bought a car for $200 in Galt, Ontario. This car had to be pushed off the lot to get it started. Dave and I picked up our last paychecks on Friday and started to head back to Montreal to party with our friends. Coming down a road towards the 401 highway, we saw a sign with arrows pointing east which was the direction we were supposed to be going and the other arrow pointing west. I stopped the car and asked Dave if we really wanted to go back home or should we point my car west and try to get on another line that we heard was kicking off in B.C. After a fifteen-second well thought out plan, we headed west towards Detroit, past Chicago, into the Dakotas and up to Winnipeg. This was a route I had not made before.

We arrived in downtown Detroit and stopped for a bite to eat. Dave saw a movie theatre with Hells Angels on Wheels playing. We walked across the street, bought two tickets and noticed a peculiar look on the ticket person's face. There were actually two movies playing, the second movie was The Ku Klux Klan. As we opened the inside door of the theatre, we noticed the first movie had already started. As we walked a few feet down the aisle looking for a seat, Dave grabbed my arm and I knew there was a problem instantly. Before I understood what was up, Dave whispered to me, saying don't you say an F...... word and to sit in the first seat we came to. We did just that and I started looking about in the dark. I noticed the place very full of people and that we were the only white people in the place.

Now Dave was much more news-oriented than I was and little more informed by reading newspapers, but even I had heard about the race riots that were taking place in Detroit and that many parts of the city had been burned during these riots. But it never crossed our minds coming into Detroit that day. We did not even get up for a leak for the whole two movies. Once the Ku Klux Klan movie started, you could hear the muttering of things like burn whitey and more such slurs throughout the rows of people. I was not as concerned as Dave was; after all I was not a racist and had nothing against coloured people. And besides we were Canadians. Even so, it was a little unnerving and after the movie it only took seconds to get into my car across the street and go. We found a safe place to park my car to sleep that night, locked the doors and had a good sleep. I slept in the front and Dave slept on the back seat.

I also remember the very long drive around Chicago; we must have driven for a couple of hours. What a huge city to drive around. A day or two later we found ourselves in the Dakotas heading north towards Winnipeg.

Now, I was driving a six cylinder four door Ford Fairlane. It had fairly good power for a full-size car. It was about midday, starting to rain and it was getting quite windy and dark. We also saw the odd bolt of lightning. Our radio was on and crackling from the weather around us. I noticed that I had pressed my gas pedal nearly to the floor and we were only going about forty-five miles an hour. The wind and rain had really started to get very bad and we both were trying to find a place to pull over and stop. We were going about thirty miles an hour now, and the wipers could not remove enough water for me to see very much at all. I was worried about getting hit in the back by another vehicle.

We finally spotted an entrance to a farm and pulled into the barnyard. Tree branches and other things were flying past us. On our radio we were catching bits of reports of barns and houses being torn apart by some tornadoes in Fargo, North Dakota, the town we had just come through. And these tornadoes were traveling north. I had the car in park and kept it running. It was getting very dark and the wind was something I had not experienced before. Dave jumped in the back seat and lay down. We locked the doors and I lay down on the front seat, hooking my arm through the steering wheel. The car was getting walloped on all sides by flying debris, and I was worried about my windshield as flying stuff was hitting it. We could feel the car rock with each gust of wind and a couple of times I thought it might blow right over. It got very scary with the noise and feeling that fantastic power bouncing our car around.

It was over fairly quickly and after a few more minutes I got out to see what damage the car had taken. The first thing I realized was that the car was no longer facing into the yard as I positioned it driving in; instead it had been turned all the way around and now faced the road by one of those powerful gusts of wind. There were a couple of dents but all the glass was intact. So we just had to drive straight ahead and back onto the highway heading towards Winnipeg.

In the back of my car, I had a five-gallon Igloo cooler that had come from one of the jobs. There were always many of them on nearly every piece of equipment and truck on most jobs for drinking water. We filled them each morning and added ice. They were very good for keeping water cold even on the hottest days, sometimes lasting two days at a time.

As we approached Brandon, Manitoba we bought a case of beer and some ice to keep it cold for the next time we would stop for the night. Well, it just happened that we drove through the night and the beer was not touched. Before we had left Ontario we had heard of a job in Kamloops B.C. and we were heading there to check it out. As we drove past Calgary and as we approached Canmore, I told Dave about the year I worked there at a logging camp for a very short time. Over the past night we had talked about and agreed on going to Banff and maybe staying in the Banff Springs Hotel for a few days. After all we were flush with cash from the last job. And we felt a little like big shots.

It was now afternoon and very hot driving even with the car windows opened, no air conditioner in those days. We were also thirsty. Dave suggested that perhaps we should have a beer from the cooler that might still be cold. Sure I said, so while I was driving, Dave reached back and grabbed two cans out of the cooler, saying they are still very cold.

He opened both cans as I was driving and we both had a very nice swallow of cold beer. We commented on how good it tasted on such a hot day. I raised mine to my lips again and right beside my car passing me was an RCMP cop car with those beautiful red flashing lights. The passenger cop pointed to me to pull over and I parked on the shoulder of the road.

Dave and I just looked at each other and knew we were done like dinner. The cop asked who was going to take responsibility for having open beer in the car and I said

I would. He not only confiscated the two in our hands, but he took the other ten beer in the cooler. He made me follow him back to their station and I could see us sitting in the single cell that was in the corner of the room. They asked us how much have you had to drink today, and we told them one mouthful. The both cops laughed at that and said, do you think I was born yesterday? I opened my wallet and found the receipt for the twelve beer I had bought in Brandon. And I asked him if he could count to twelve. He took ten out of the cooler and we had one each in our hands. The older cop looked at his buddy and said, I don't think this kid was born yesterday either. They both had a laugh and told me there was going to be a fine of $20 or we could see the judge in the morning. I quickly gave him $20 and he did give me a receipt for it, and we were on our way again.

Before we got to Banff, Dave and I bought two cases of twenty-four beer to have at the hotel over a couple days. We pulled up in front of the Banff Springs Hotel and a fellow wearing a kilt and a pompom hat opened the doors of this old and dented car. He asked to take our bags, and Dave and I carried the two cases of beer into the hotel as another fellow parked the car for us. We must have been a sight, wearing our western cowboy boots, jeans, jean jackets and we wore brightly coloured and sometimes floral western shirts. All pipeliners dressed that way. And carrying two cases of beer to the check-in desk.

Once in our room, we found out that the staff of these CPR hotels were mostly university students from across Canada working for the summer. We had a lot of traffic coming into our room for a beer over the next few days. Even the elevator operators would dash in for a quick cold one when they got to our floor. We had a pretty good time playing the high rollers for a few days before we left for Kamloops to see if that job had kicked off yet. It had not,

Looking cool in Banff. Another road-trip.

and Dave decided he'd had enough of pipelining work and took the train back to Montreal.

I caught wind of a pipeline contract that had just been awarded and the company that was setting up a yard in Quesnel B.C., so I headed north up the Okanogan valley to Quesnel. Beautiful country. It was now autumn and I was enjoying my drive along the river when I spotted a single fellow on a sandbar that was close to the far side of the river. He seemed to be working at something over there and I pulled over to see if I could tell what he might be doing. After a moment or two I saw that he was panning gold and I also saw him shoveling gravel into a small wooden slew. I had never seen that kind of work done before, except in the old western movies. I watched for a few minutes before I decided to go over to speak to him. I wondered if a living could be made at this. So I rolled up my pants and started to wade across. I have no idea why I rolled up my pants because by the time I was in the middle of the river the water was above my belt. As I walked on the sand bar towards this fellow who looked to be native and very well on in years, he never raised his head from his work. After a short time I said hello with no response. I stood there for a short time and he never acknowledged my presence. Feeling a little uncomfortable and stupid, I said, have a nice day, and I waded back over to my car. I wondered if he could not speak English, or was a mute or something else.

I continued on to Quesnel, some fifteen or twenty more miles up river. Very soon on the main street in town I spotted a pipeline surveyor's truck parked on the street with a fellow inside it. I asked him where the company yard was located, and he told me. So I headed a short distance out of town to the yard. When I got there, only the office, a few trucks and a few trailers were there. I went to the office and spoke to one of the men at his desk. I asked when their job was going to kick off and he told me they were only going to start in the spring. I asked him to remember me and that I would be in their yard for work in the spring. I asked permission to sleep in their yard that night in my car. He pointed to an area and told me I could park there for the night.

With money in short supply and winter approaching, I had to come up with some kind of a job in short order. Now Quesnel had a sawmill at one end of town and a Dairy Queen at the other with a few stores and small businesses between. I knocked on every door and no one had need of any help. I went back to the yard that night and had permission again to park my car for the night. I had the idea of heading back south looking for work along the way and then east to Calgary and maybe winter there.

In the morning I headed down river until I again came to the spot that I had waded across the river to check out the old prospector. And there he was again, working away.

Well I have to tell you, my next move was one of the best decisions I ever made.

CHAPTER

8

A Winter in Joe's Cabin

A t the river, I decided to wade back over to where the old prospector was working. But I used a different strategy this time. Once I got to where he was working, I stayed back a ways and found a stone to sit on and watch. Not a word passed between us for a couple hours. He stopped working, opened his lunch bucket and ate his lunch, then went back to work. As he was at the water's edge panning, I walked over and picked up his shovel. I dug exactly where I had watched him dig, and I started to put gravel into his slew for him. I was not sure if I was going to receive something across the side of my head or not. But as it turned out for the rest of the day I worked the slew and he did the panning. He did not say very much to me but I found out he was half French and half Native and went by the name Joe.

I slept in my car again that night and I asked Joe if I could help him again tomorrow so I could learn from him. He said okay and he told me he would bring me something for my lunch.

Joe had a log cabin on that far bank about a quarter mile in the woods. He told me he built the cabin himself in his younger years. The outside of his cabin was covered with all kinds of animal traps, snares, hand-made snowshoes, and different rigging. He had a hip roof from one side of the cabin where he had many cords of dry stove wood piled.

He also had a log shed filled with more tools and supplies. He had an outhouse behind the cabin on a couple of large logs overhanging a small ravine. His water came from the river. He had a large old cast iron wood stove for heat and to cook on. He had a root cellar under a door in the floor of the cabin where he stored most of his food.

I asked if it would be possible for me to stay and help him until I went to work for the pipeline in the spring. I stayed at Joe's cabin for about five months. We put together a steel framed bed for me and I used my sleeping bag that I always had in my car along with my pillow and a couple of blankets that I always had with me.

We caught fish in the river and had some great fish dinners at the cabin. When the river started to freeze, gold season ended and his trapping season started. Joe said that he could not pay me, but if I wanted to trap with him that year, he would feed me and I would be warm for the winter. I would also be right handy to Quesnel for the spring pipeline kick off that I had told Joe about. So we had a deal. This trapping business and being in the woods sounded pretty exciting to me. I was so looking forward to it for sure.

After gold season, Joe started to gather the supplies that he was going to need for his trapline season from around the cabin. He liked the way I could sharpen skinning knives as I had learned to do at the carpenters' trade school in Montreal. He started to gain more and more confidence in me as time went on. He talked very little but when he did I knew to pay attention to whatever he said. He took me with him as we went out on the two trapline paths that he went on every day during the trapping season. One went to the right of the cabin for about seven miles. And the other one went to the left of the cabin about the same distance. There were only a couple inches of snow on the ground at that time. He was looking for signs of wildlife and we cleared the trail of dead wood that had fallen on the trail over the year. I watched Joe intently as he read the forest floor and surroundings. His hearing was impeccable as he would hear things that I could not. This was the first time that I realized I had poor hearing. Joe showed me how to make many different kinds of trap sets. And how to bait each one for the many species that we were trying to catch.

Once the snow built up on the ground, Joe gave me a pair of snowshoes that he had made out of alder branch, flexible and strong. He had two truck engine hoods that when upside down made great toboggans. We had a rope affixed from each side of the hood that we put around the back of our necks, under our armpits and these hoods slid along the snow with ease with us towing them. Every morning we loaded each hood or toboggan with all the supplies that we would need for a day of trapping. Bait, traps, hatchets and everything else. Both of his trapline trails he checked every second day. He would set and harvest a trail one day and the next day the other trail. When we came back to the cabin each night with our catch still in the round, we could be pulling a few hundred pounds each of animals caught that day.

Once we were back, we took them into the cabin and spread them out on the floor to thaw while we had our supper. And by the way, I never knew what I was eating because we always ate what we caught, and all the meat looked similar. Joe did most of the cooking. Every meal was delicious.

After our supper we would start skinning everything that we had caught that day. Beaver, marten, lynx, bobcat, fox, mink, muskrat, raccoon, the odd wolf and wolverine. I was very good at keeping all the skinning knives razor sharp. I soon found out how important it was to have super sharp knives. I learned something new every day. We then rolled up the skins tightly, put as many that would fit into burlap bags and piled them in a firmly built log box outside the cabin to stay frozen until trapping season was finished. The smell of the hides from around that box would surely attract bears once out of hibernation and other critters too. So now I understood why this box was made like Fort Knox. Then we would start fleshing the skins, scraping off the fat from the hide, and pinning them onto boards to dry.

One day heading back to the cabin after a very successful and full day, I was following Joe's sled, pulling mine. I might have had two hundred pounds on my sled. It was toward the end of the season. Days were getting longer and it was getting warmer, with the snow getting stickier. I was sweating bullets pulling supplies and fur still in the round out of the wood and having a hard time keeping up to this old fellow, Joe. I thought to myself, as my heart was pounding in my chest trying to keep up to Joe, that there must be a better way to produce and harvest fur domestically for market.

I kept that thought and expanded on it in my mind over the next few years, thinking about how one day I might be able to build a fur operation. I learned an awful lot from Joe. And after I had become quite successful many years later, I went back to his cabin and Quesnel to see if he might still be around someplace in a home or something. His cabin had been abandoned for a long time and one side had buckled. I never met anyone around the area or Quesnel who knew what had happened to him. I expect to see you one day in heaven, Joe.

CHAPTER
9
A Romance and a Heartbreak

That spring after leaving Joe I drove back to Quesnel to find out when this pipeline was kicking off and to find out which foremen were going to be working that job. I was surprised to see a couple of people that I had previously worked with already in the yard. Machinery was being hauled in and parked in the yard daily. I asked around for work and was given a boom truck. This is a flatbed three-ton truck with two steel poles that tucked into the side of the deck when not being used. When the poles were erect and always attached to the end of the deck, they formed a fifteen foot high vee formation boom and had a pulley on top. There is a winch on the deck behind the cab and that cable would thread through the pulley. This boom truck was used for many things. It would lift and carry heavy water pumps around where needed. It could pick up and move just about anything. I would drive to Prince George picking up supplies for the upcoming job and unload into the different parts and supply trailers in the yard. Everyday there was something different to do with this truck. And I would get my marching orders each morning.

I asked for a small advance on my pay and checked into the only hotel in Quesnel. The hotel soon filled up with pipeliners. I only knew a few from past jobs. A lot of us ate breakfast at the same diner across the street from the hotel, and I had them make a couple sandwiches for my lunch pail everyday. Driving this boom truck I never knew where I might be working so I always had a little grub and water with me. Like every pipeline job we worked seven days a week from sunup to dark most days.

This particular job starting up went very well. The right away and surrounding area was mostly on high ground. So things dried out quickly. Every crew was making good progress and we were covering a lot of finished pipe.

In the beer lounge of the hotel where every night the men would sit, talk and have a few pints, there was a very nice-looking girl walking around the tables selling cigarettes, nuts, gum and other items. She carried all these items on a tray in front of her held up by a ribbon around her neck. She was blonde and wore a blue costume, frilled skirt and blouse. Over a few weeks I got to have a few chats with her as she worked every night at the hotel. I found out her name was Karyn and that she was separated from a husband in Edmonton who was violent towards her and her two children. The boy was six and her little girl was five.

I asked her where her children were and she told me they were at a motel a few blocks away where she was living and that her older brother who was a full blown alcoholic was taking care of them while she was trying to make a buck for all of them. I watched her as she worked at times around all these men and I liked the way she carried herself. Always a smile, and all business. Not flirtatious, just very pleasant with everyone. Watching her, she reminded me of the different ways that I had to sell things trying to earn money, years earlier.

When pipelining we hardly ever had a day off. But this coming Sunday we were not going to be working, for some reason that I do not remember. Karyn did not work Sundays. So rather than just sit around the bar with the boys on the day off, I asked Karyn if I could pick her and her two kids up and take them to the Dairy Queen Sunday afternoon. She said she would give it some thought. Now it took a lot for me to muster up the nerve to ask her as I was not your average ladies' man. I sure liked them well enough. But I was very shy and had far too many inferiority complexes in those days.

But after some time, Karyn came back to my table to say that it would be very nice of me to want to take her family out for a few hours. I was very thrilled and I looked forward to Sunday.

Sunday I was right on time going to her motel to pick them up. I stepped inside and met the kids and her brother. Who I could tell, was a big time boozer and I wondered how well he took care of the kids when she was at work. And I was glad that she had not asked him along. We had a grand day; after leaving the Dairy Queen we found a small playground where I had a little fun with the kids and had a short drive along the river. I had a nice day and her kids were great.

About four weeks or so following that Sunday, Karyn informed me that her brother was leaving and going to Vancouver and she thought she was going to have to quit her job. I also knew that my company yard was moving up the line to Prince George, as the work was getting very close to that city now. Over the months Karyn and I talked a lot together. I enjoyed little bits of time with her a lot more than sitting with the boys pounding the pints. I could never keep up to the heavy drinking anyway. After her work one night we sat at a table talking and I told her that I never would know the day that I would have to pack up and move up to Prince George. But I asked her if she might be interested in moving up there with me. I had had a welder friend of mine already moved to a motel in Prince George book one of the motel units for me. The next day she told me that she had talked to her kids about the idea. And told me the kids liked me and that she thought it could work out. I think she was about five years older than I was, but I never asked.

Not long after that I had her drive my car up to Prince George as I had my boom truck to take. We piled into the motel, and I had an instant family and for the first time someone to come home to. It was marvelous. Karyn and me, Albert and Annette as well as one Siamese cat.

A lot of the men stayed at this motel and also had their wives and families with them. Karyn fit right in with them making friends. I was so proud and happy that she would take a chance on me. I was going to do my very best to provide for them. They needed me and I sure needed them. Maybe not the cat though.

All the men were putting in a lot of hours all summer, and we were nearing the end of this job in a few weeks. We sat around in the evening talking about which pipeline jobs were coming up next. Some were planning to go to a couple of jobs in the States. There was another camp job for winter work. Another was already being built across the St Lawrence River in Boucherville, Quebec. Right beside St. Lambert.

One evening we were in our motel. I was watching the news and Karyn was reading a bedtime story to the kids. There was a loud knock on our door and I answered it thinking it was one of my motel neighbors. A great big rough-looking fellow put one foot into my room and bellowed at me, You got my kids in there. Instantly the kids ran across the hallway and into the bathroom locking the door. That was all I needed to see before picking up the phone and dialing 0 for the motel office. I knew the motel owner very well and I told him to get the cops over here right now. I put down the phone and stood in this fellow's way. Behind him was an older women yelling that they were her grandkids. I tried to talk and stall while Karyn stayed in the bedroom and the kids were locked in the bathroom. The motel manager arrived as well, telling this big fellow that the police were on their way. I felt better with a little support and I asked him to step back outside just as the cops came in. They asked who everyone was and I piped up first saying that this is my residence and I wanted these two people removed, pointing at the big fellow and his mother. The cops took them outside and came right back to my door, wanting to see the kids who were still locked in the bathroom. Karyn and I talked the kids out and the cops asked them and Karyn a couple of questions. The cops were now understanding of the situation and went back outside to talk to Karyn's husband and mother-in-law.

After a while both officers came back to our room and warned us that their plan was to grab the kids. That night after the kids were sleeping, we talked about what to do. I had to go to work in the morning and she would be alone with the kids at the motel. I went next door to mine, where my friend the welder and his wife lived and told them what all the commotion was about. I asked his wife if she might stay with Karyn the next day while I was at work. She and Karyn got along well as it was.

The next day I spoke to my boss after lunch and he had already heard of my problem. He told me that this job was nearly done if I wanted my drag up check. I asked to use his phone and I called the St. Lambert recreation department to speak to the fellow that I had worked for twice before in the winter taking care of a chalet and outdoor rink. His name was Eric Sharp. I told Eric that I now had a family and was finishing up my work in B.C. Would he hire me for this upcoming winter again? He said no problem, see you in November. I only had about two more weeks left of work on this job and I asked for my check. I thanked my boss and told him I would like to work again for him someday. I went back to the motel and told Karyn that I had just quit my job and that I had a job for the winter in

Quebec. We did not tell anyone where we were headed. We packed everything into the car, said our goodbyes and left for Montreal.

Now I always hid and covered up from everyone the fact I could not read or write and Karyn had no idea either.

On that drive across the country, we talked about marriage, how she could get a divorce and how I might adopt her kids. I was coming back to my hometown as being a shacked up couple which was frowned on big time back then. I wanted Karyn and the kids to be received well by my friends and family. So we stopped in Kenora, Ontario and bought two cheap wedding rings. I phoned my mother from Kenora and said that I had married a ready made family and I had a job to go to when I got back to St. Lambert. But I needed a place to stay for one or two days until we found an apartment close to schools for my kids. She said that would be alright and was anxious to meet my family.

We did stay three days and I found an apartment in Greenfield Park on Churchill Boulevard. It was walking distance to school and shopping. My friends helped me get some furniture and I got a double bed from my folks. I bought bunk beds for the kids and everything seemed to fall into place.

It was now a week before school started for Albert and Annette. We registered them and got them some clothes and school supplies. After they started school, Karyn and I took a drive to this river pipeline that I had heard was in full swing in Boucherville on the river upstream from St. Lambert and Greenfield Park. This line was being constructed in a very unique way. I walked over to the office and asked if they had anything for me to do, and they did. One of the welder's helpers had just gone back to university and he needed a helper. I started work the very next day.

Now this line that was going across the two-mile wide St. Lawrence River was not a single line, but a triple line. A little offshore was an island and there were train tracks put across from the shore and across this island. All along the one-mile length of track there were small rail cars about eight feet square, staggered. Skids were piled on each one of the rail cars that the three pipelines side by side were being constructed and welded on top of. Once all the pipes were completed, we would cap all the ends and a river tugboat would hook onto one line at a time and float it across the river to be connected to the far shore with the other end lifted up onto a barge anchored in the river. Then the tug boat pulled the second line out to the barge in the river and we welded onto the first section. That pipe's other end was put up on another barge closer to our shore to be welded together to the last pipe still on the rails.

The dredges had previously dug the trench in the bottom of the river to accommodate the constructed pipeline. We then sank the pipe into the trench by filling it with water. Once the one-ton cement river weights were affixed around the pipe in the trench, the water was blown out of the pipe using compressed air. Then the pipeline could continue being built across the countryside on both sides of the river.

I had about two months work on this line before reporting to the St. Lambert recreation department for my winter job taking care of a chalet, shoveling snow, making and maintaining the ice rink.

It was a very exciting time for me. I had a ready made family to show off and care for. Things were going well. Karyn got to meet some of my friends who we went with to house parties. My parents liked and were grandparents to Annette and Albert. The kids liked school and I had a great time taking them to see Santa and different places. It was a wonderful winter. It was the first time the kids ever saw a

Santa Claus parade. I remember well having Annette sitting on my shoulders watching the parade and warming my neck and back as she wet her pants. Karyn use to drop me off at the rink for work and she took the car for the day. We had a very nice Christmas and I bought them all their first skates and taught them to skate at the rink that I took care of. I finally had what I always wanted the most in life, a family.

Starting a new family like this took a fair bit of money but I did not mind, it was an investment for our future. I knew that I only had a low pay part-time job that was going to end as spring arrived. I knew I needed to find a good full-time job somewhere so I started looking. I didn't really want to go pipelining some place and leave them behind. I wanted a home life.

In early spring about the time my rink job with the city was ended, I noticed our phone bill for April was a little heavy and there was a number in Calgary that seemed to be frequently called. I asked Karyn about it and she told me it was her niece who was single and had just given birth to her first child a few months earlier.

A few weeks later I happened to come home and had to get to the bathroom quickly. While I was in the bathroom the phone rang and Karyn answered, not knowing that I had come home and was sitting in the bathroom. I overheard pretty much most of the conversation. She was saying to some person that she has gone to the welfare people here, and that they are paying for her three train tickets back to Alberta. She said that they would leave Quebec as soon as the kids were out of school in a couple weeks. I waited for her to hang up the phone and I came out of the bathroom as if nothing was wrong. I asked her who had called and she said it was her niece again from Calgary. The next question from me was, is everything alright?

She said yes, her niece called just wanting some advice on medicine for her baby or something. The two kids had just come home and I needed a little time to think. So I never said a word about the phone call until the kids were in bed. Then I asked her if she was going for a visit because I had heard something about tickets to Alberta in a couple weeks.

She started by saying, I was going to tell you, but did not know how. She said that she was going back to Alberta and moving into half of a house with her niece and baby. The two of them would live on welfare out there and split the expenses. Karyn said she was homesick for the west and she did not speak French and did not want to live where she could not understand the language spoken.

I told her I was disappointed in her and that I was very pissed off for her making plans and not telling me. I did not know what I might have done and could we come up with a solution? My head was whirling and I just could not figure this out. I was very confused and panicking.

It is not you, it is me, she said. I did not want to hurt you she said.

Hurt me? Your killing me, I said. Have I done something wrong? I was in disbelief that this was happening. I tried to suggest alternatives but her mind was made up. She did not ask for a cent, and told me the welfare was taking care of everything. I knew nothing about welfare, but she sure knew her way around it well. By the second week of June they were gone. I hugged the kids and told them I would always love them.

Now, what was I supposed to tell my parents and friends? After all we were married, right. They were my family. Right! I had lied and deceived people and now I had to face the music. I did not know what to tell anyone; I didn't even know what had happened myself. I was about to find out.

Not long after Karyn and the kids had arrived in Alberta, I received a letter from her. It said that things didn't work out with her niece and she had found a very nice basement apartment in Calgary and was now living there. Would I be willing to come out there? The kids missed me. I tore it up and never answered her letter.

Now the car that I bought for $200 when I was with Dave was just about fried, after serving me very well for a couple years. The engine went on it and I scrapped it. Around that time I happened to be sitting in my apartment in Greenfield Park with one of my pipeline friends, Pete Thompson. He was going to a pipeline job in northern Alberta in a few weeks. He had been hired as a lowboy truck driver. It was only going to be about two-month job. Would I be interested in splitting gas and motel and going with him in his half-ton truck to that job and back? And we would get a couple of months pay. I told him no because I was not guaranteed a job when I got there. And I had just lined up a job working at the harbour.

Two weeks went by and another letter arrived from Calgary. It had a phone number for me to call. It was from Karyn again, asking for a second time if I could come out there and things would work out for us. And she also told me that she was pregnant with my child.

Now that changed things big time for me. I am not one to bring a child into this world and not be there for it. I phoned her that minute and wanted to verify what she had written me. My reading was not very good. I told her that if I went out to her, I might even have a job to go to northwest of Edmonton but that I would get back to her because I did not have a car any longer.

I phoned my friend Pete Thompson and asked him if he still intended to go to the job in Alberta. He told me he was leaving in three days. I asked him that if I phoned the yard office and got a job, could we load bunk beds and some of my other furniture onto his truck and drop it off at Karyn's place in Calgary on the way up to the job.

I phoned the pipeline contractor. I told them I was driving out there with Pete Thompson, who they knew very well. Pete had worked for them on a few occasions before. I asked if when I got out there, was there any chance of a job for me to do. And I said that I needed work. They said I could work in the warehouse parts supply trailer when I got there.

So Pete and I got busy, getting our gear together and we built a small wood frame to box in the back of his truck and covered the top and sides with plastic. We loaded everything and hit the road for Calgary. With both of us driving we covered a lot of ground quickly. We drove night and day. One of us slept as the other drove.

When Pete and I arrived in Calgary we found the house easily. It was very nice, larger than most and a newer home. I wondered how she could afford it. She told me that the government welfare department was paying for it. I did not know anything about welfare. The basement had two large bedrooms and a smaller one, a living room, kitchen and dining area and bathroom.

And as I got out of the truck the two kids came running out of the house to greet me. It was nice to hug them again. Karyn came outside as well, with a big smile and I could see at once she was very pregnant. I could not get over how big she was and I asked her when her date was. She said late November. I said good, I would not want to miss being there then with you. I told her that I would be back from the job before then for sure. We unloaded all the furniture and brought it downstairs. We put up the kids' bunk beds for them first thing. Even the home owners who lived upstairs gave a hand. Pete slept on the couch that night and we planned to leave for the job site first thing in the morning. Karyn and I had a lot of talking and planning to do before we left next morning. Karyn told me she was living on welfare. I told her that I would be back in two months or so, and that welfare would not be necessary anymore. I would find work in Calgary.

After sleeping a cozy night with her and my first child that I was getting very excited about having, Pete and I had a bit of breakfast and left early in the morning for work up north.

The job site was located northwest of Edmonton. All the way past Hinton. We first reported to the office and then we found a motel room. Again we worked seven days a week and ten to twelve hours a day. We were on time and a half overtime pay rate by Thursday and made very good money. I would need every cent once I got back to Karyn, so I never spent a cent on anything except for the motel room and food. I never drank a single beer the whole job I remember.

One of the fellows who worked in the main office trailer had just bought a brand new truck and wanted to sell his car that he had parked at the motel where we stayed. It was an Austen Cambridge station wagon, with low mileage and in perfect shape. I knew I would need a car when I got back to Calgary. It was a standard gear shift that I knew Karyn could drive and I liked it. So I bought it for a very decent price. That I cannot remember.

Once this job was finished, both Pete and I had done very well monetarily. Pete was then asked that on his way home east would he drive his company tractor trailer to North Battleford, Saskatchewan, with a small office trailer loaded and drop both off there. Pete loaded his own half-ton truck on the deck as well and he left on his way. I called Karyn and headed back to my family in Calgary, driving my car.

When I got to Karyn's place, the kids were in school and the woman who lived upstairs and owned the house was sitting having a cup of tea with Karyn. I got a very nice hug and I joined their conversation. Apparently the welfare people had just visited that morning and had laid out some rules to Karyn about the conditions for her to continue receiving welfare. One of them was that she had to only be living there with the two kids. Well, I said, we don't need that bloody welfare anymore now anyway.

The next morning, Karyn was saying that I would have to find another place to stay, just until the baby was born. Karyn was only a few weeks away from having the baby and I did not want to cause any upset. She also knew the way things worked with these welfare people a lot better than I did. We talked some and I said I would get a room at the YMCA, to alleviate any potential problem with these welfare people. I would start looking for a permanent job right away. Once I had a job we could get clear of these welfare people for good. So I took a room at the downtown Y. I would go to her place nearly every day. We often took the car and bought things for the new arrival. Crib, bassinet, and a host of other items. We started to buy Christmas presents for Albert and Annette as well.

The head office of a very large pipeline company was just outside of the city. In the winter all the trucks and bulldozers and other equipment were stored there. All the permanent working mechanics, welders and others worked all winter there. They would tear down and rebuild motors and all the equipment to get ready for the upcoming year.

I went to see them about a job and fortunately I met a couple of men who I had worked with before. I was given an 8am to 5pm salary job. I was a parts chaser for them. I was given a half-ton truck with a radio in it. I would drive all over the city picking up all the parts and supplies for the repair work being done in the main shop. It was a great job and they told me they would keep me on at that location all year if I wanted. I was thrilled. And I told Karyn that after the baby came, we could start looking for a home. I went over there or called her every day.

One night after work I arrived back at the Y, had a shower and phoned Karyn as I did most nights to talk or go over there. No answer. I called again around 9pm, and still no answer. I thought it strange. In the morning, 6am being too early to call disturbing her much needed sleep, I left for work. At lunch time I called her, and again no answer. Now I was getting concerned. After work again I called from the YMCA, and it was her upstairs lady friend that picked up the phone. She was babysitting the kids and I asked where Karyn was. Oh she said, she is not home from the hospital yet, she had a baby girl.

All excited I showered, got dressed, hopped in my car and raced to the hospital. I picked up a bunch of flowers on the way. I got to the maternity ward and could hardly contain my excitement as I spoke to the nurse at the counter. I introduced myself and told her who I was here to see. She walked me to a room and told me to sit down and that she would be back shortly. In the room there were about three other fellows and, me being a social person, I struck up a conversation almost immediately. They were all new fathers. One fellow's wife was in the delivery room as we spoke. I bragged that my wife had my first daughter the day before and that I was there to see them.

A few minutes later the nurse came to get me and took me into the hallway. She first asked a question. Are you the putative father? Not having any idea what that word meant I just said yes. She then told me that Karyn did not want to see me at this time. Being totally blown away and embarrassed by this, I shoved my flowers at her saying, "Okay then, just give her these for me, please", and I bolted for the elevator. On my drive back to the YMCA in total bewilderment, I thought that this must be those bloody welfare people causing her to act this way. And that I had better stay away from the hospital and wait for her to get home with my daughter.

I parked my car at the Y and headed for the bar down the street. If I was going to sleep that night I needed a few. I pounded a couple into me and went back to the Y to bed.

The next day at work I told everyone there that I was now a father of a new baby daughter and I handed out a few cigars. One of the ladies in the office said Karyn might be in the hospital for a couple days.

I wanted to go to the house each evening after work to check if Karyn was home yet. But I stayed away in case those welfare people were there. A day or two later, I phoned Karyn's place and the babysitter told me she was coming home the next day. I told her to tell Karyn that I would be over after work the next day.

After work that day, I went over to the house to find a lot of people there. Some of Karyn's family members were gathered around her and the baby. Everyone was celebrating and happy.

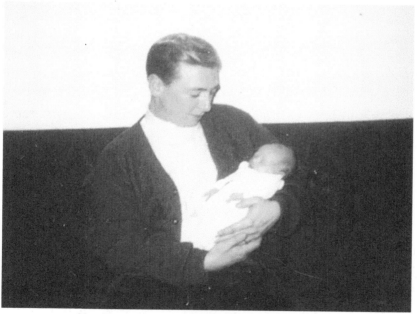

Me with my daughter Shannon just after she was born.
Sadly, I lost her and would not find her again for many years.

My daughter's name was Shannon Pearl and I thought the last name was going to be Cobb. I found out later it was not.

At one point Karyn asked if I wanted to hold the baby and of course I said yes. So I sat in the living room on the couch and Karyn's sister Pearl gave me Shannon to hold for the first time.

I was well aware of how genetics worked in birds and animals and I remember very well looking at Shannon as I held her for the very first time, saying to her that I prayed she did not inherit any of the defects that I knew I had. I had no idea what they were, but I knew I had them.

I remember this like yesterday. Most everyone else was gathered around Karyn in the kitchen. Albert and Annette were sitting on both sides of me on the couch. I asked them how they liked their new sister. Of course they were thrilled. But what Albert said to me while I was holding her blew me right out of the water. Albert told me that Shannon was going to be given to his Aunt Pearl. I did not know what to think.

He said that Mom was giving baby Shannon to her sister Pearl because Aunt Pearl could not have kids of her own. I asked Albert a few questions as we sat together on the couch and he told me that this was Mom's and Aunt Pearl's plan for a long time. That is why Shannon received the middle name Pearl. I told Albert not to tell anyone what he had told me. It would be our secret. Another blown out of the water moment for me. Could this be true? I was not even sure if Albert knew what he was talking about. So I did not say a thing about what I had learned to anyone. The rest of my time there that evening, I looked at Karyn and her sister Pearl for any sign that might suggest Albert's story was true. My imagination was playing games with my head, I thought. I felt very uncomfortable and decided to leave. I had to go to work next morning.

All the next day at work I tried to figure out if I was dreaming or just being delusional or something. I was going to go to the house after work again that night. But how would I bring up such a subject to her. I started to think back when Karyn left me in Greenfield Park. The phone calls back and forth from Calgary. Could these calls been between Pearl and Karyn all along?

I knew that I had always had a hard time to understand things, so was I imagining these things? Or could it be possible that any person was that cruel and capable of pulling the wool over my eyes like this? I just could not believe it to be true. So I tried to just ignore this stupid inclination that I was imagining. But I said to myself that if it was true I would one day find her!

When I arrived at the YMCA after work, the desk clerk told me there were two gentlemen sitting in the lobby who needed to talk to me. I turned to see who it might be and they were already approaching me. I was in my work grubbies and they were wearing suit, and overcoats. They introduced themselves by their names and said they were from some agency or something. They said that they had a private matter to discuss with me and could we talk in private in my room. I said sure and we went up to my small room. I sat on my bed with one of them and the other sat on my wood chair. I had no idea who these guys were.

The fellow sitting on the chair opened a small briefcase and first handed me a business card. I could see it had the Alberta flag in the corner of it. So I knew they were government persons. He started to talk about me fathering a child and started to tell me that I was responsible for child support and wanted to know how much money I made and how much a month I was going to pay the government. I told him to back up a minute and I said that Karyn and I were planning to get married and get a house together. I was even going to adopt her other two children.

The more this fellow talked, the more I realized that the only way they had all that information about us living in Quebec together and where I lived now, my name, birthdate, and where I worked et cetera was from Karyn.

The fellow produced papers that he told me I'd have to sign before he left. I already saw on the papers a figure and dollar sign. He also said that if I refused to sign these papers, he had the authority to have me taken into custody and hold me overnight for the judge in the morning.

Well, I guess I needed that for some vivid clarity. Now for the very first time I understood I had been played for the fool that I was, big time.

I sure understood the situation that I found myself in and now remembered all the way back to the phone calls in the apartment in Greenfield Park. It was never the niece calling Karyn; it was sister Pearl. A cold sweat came over me, with these guys in my room. Nobody was taking me to jail for the night. What if Shannon was not even mine, I thought? I knew what I had to do. I went into a con mode and became very compliant and friendly. Saying no problem, I pretended to read the papers and then I said okay, where do I sign. I also kept talking about how things were going to correct themselves and how Karyn and I were going to have a great family life as soon as we found a house to purchase. I kept yapping and distracting them as he pointed to the place for me to sign his papers. I scribbled down something, not my name for sure. I shook their hands and they left my room. I looked out my window waiting to see them get into their car in the parking lot. I thought it odd that they would park beside mine. I thought they would have written down my plate number. Again knowing that Karyn would be the only one to tell them what my car looked like.

It took me less than an hour to pack my things and put everything into my car. I was a complete emotional mess by this point. How could I have been so stupid and believed everything she told me? I now knew for sure that I was only just a meal ticket for her. Going all the way back to when I met her in Quesnel the year before.

I then phoned my boss at home, who I got along fantastically well with. I told him I had an emergency and that I had to travel to Vancouver first thing in the morning. Would he be able to have my drag up check ready for me first thing in the morning? He said no problem. And he asked if I would be coming back to work. I told him I did not think so and I thanked him very kindly for the work that he had given me.

I slept very poorly that night at the Y. The next morning as I was picking up my paycheck from my boss, I told him I was headed west to Vancouver because that was the opposite way I was going to drive and I did not want the police to be stopping me on the road. I intended to go east heading back to Montreal. Those guys had made me feel like I was some kind of a criminal and I had no idea what they might do If they found out I had left Calgary. I cashed my check at the bank twenty minutes after receiving it. I gassed up my car and took off for the Saskatchewan border. My mind was playing tricks as I saw every car behind me as a cop car.

All the way back to Montreal I asked myself many questions. Why did God make me this way? I was always having such a troubled life.

I always wanted to please; I wanted to do the right thing. How was it that I could not understand things the way others did? I always had to hide the fact that I was defective by bullshitting people. Creating more trouble for myself. I was feeling totally worthless and I now knew I was never going to have a normal life like others. Or have a family life like all the other people I knew. Especially now going back to Quebec to live. How would I ever get work there, I could not speak enough French, and I could not even read or write in English but for a few words. I was so distraught, and I could not understand how anyone could do such a thing.

I was of the opinion at the time that it was men who were the cheaters and schemers of life and most women were kind, gentle, loving and giving. Now I knew that this was another misconception of mine. This was not the case at all. I also understood now why some men become violent towards some women. This is something I could never do or understand. I was taught very differently. It took a very long time before I fully trusted a woman again.

A lot of tears dripped onto my shirt driving back east across the country. I worked my way out of this funk, by telling myself that I was only feeling sorry for myself and to give my head a shake. I had not done anything wrong and I was the one who had been screwed over.

I told myself that if Shannon was mine. I would someday find her and try to explain why I was not able to be around in her life. I also started to come out of this funk thinking about different ways that I might be able to get back on my feet other than working pipeline. I was tired of running all over the country from one town to another. Being laid off after each contract finished. Tired of hotel rooms and eating in diners. I told myself I had to make it a different way. But how?

Everything went through my mind. I even thought of maybe making a withdrawal from a bank using a note. I had a little chuckle to myself. First I was too chicken to pull off something like that, and second, who would write the note for me to give the teller? I thought of all kinds of crazy stuff on that drive home.

Leaving Alberta, it was terribly cold, now December. My car did not have snow tires and my heater was not working for some reason. I had a blanket around my legs, toque, gloves, boots and coat on. My windshield had to be scraped inside from frost every few minutes to see out. As soon as I got to Saskatchewan. I stopped at the first truck stop on the highway and I asked for a mechanic. They told me that my radiator thermostat was a summer one and I needed a winter one installed. It took them most of the day to find one for me and get me back on the road. After paying for that work, I figured that I might be able to afford two nights in a motel on this trip and just have enough money for gas and food to get back to Montreal. I had been working but also giving most of my money to Karyn.

It was the worst drive of my life. With summer tires on my car, it was just a matter of time before I was going to run into bad roads and be stuck someplace. I had good weight with all my stuff in the car. But it was a white knuckle drive for sure. As soon as I arrived in Manitoba, I found myself in a winter blizzard. I started to look for a motel and soon found out that all the motels were full. I had left it too late to get off the highway. I was having a terrible time keeping momentum with summer tires on the car.

I caught up to a transport truck that I could hardly see in front of me from the snow he was kicking up. I kept my left side tires in his tracks and followed him as closely as I dared to; I also used his draft from being behind him. My right side tires had to make their own way through the snow. This went on for many, many miles until I spotted a large motel sign saying vacancy, (you see I could read some words) and I turned in. I checked in, ate and went to sleep. I must have slept for twelve hours straight and did I ever need it. I had been totally emotionally spent the past two days. I'm not sure what a nervous breakdown is or supposed to feel like. But I am sure I was there.

The highway had been well plowed by the time I pulled back onto it next day. I knew that I had a long way to go with summer tires on. I had to drive more slowly than normal for me. I could not risk hitting a snowbank without money for even a tow truck, especially going around Kenora and Lake Superior and Northern Ontario. I cannot remember in what town I took my next motel room but it was late evening and the road was not the best to be driving at night. Another good sleep as I seemed to be able to leave my troubles further behind.

I do remember arriving back in Montreal. It was sunny and a mild morning. I was now driving in morning rush hour traffic on the Decarie Expressway, better known as the Decarie pit, and I was heading for the Champlain Bridge to the south shore and St. Lambert. I remember running out of windshield washer. The slush and tire spray was horrific and the sun made vision very dangerous. But I made it to my parents' home in St. Lambert on the south shore from Montreal. I knew they were probably at work by now.

After ringing the doorbell a few times, I went to the nail at the end of the side window sill of the porch, looking for the house key that had always hung there many years before. No key!

So now what? I walked around to the side of the house to one of the smaller wooden basement windows. I pried the wood window open with tools that I had in my car and I went in.

I opened the front door and brought in a few of my things. I noticed the artificially small Christmas tree in the living room where there had always been a well decorated real tree each year when we were kids. There was not one gift under the tree yet, it was only the first week of December or so.

I made a piece of toast and took a piece of cheese. After eating that, I took my things upstairs to my old bedroom. There were four bedrooms upstairs. The only doors open were my parents' master bedroom and the bathroom. It was about noon now and I closed my bedroom door and climbed into bed. When I woke up I had no idea of the time of day. But when I came out of my room it was daylight and I was a little confused as to the time and even where I was. It was close to mid-morning and no one was home. I had slept right through my parents coming home from work, going to bed, getting up in the morning and going back to work, without them even knowing I was asleep in the house.

I had not even phoned them to tell them I would be arriving. I did not want to answer a lot of questions on the phone. They knew Karyn was pregnant and also knew that it was the reason I went back to Alberta.

I spent the day mostly in the house, but I thought I would surprise them with supper for the three of us when they got home from work. So I went out and bought some pork chops, they had potatoes, so I made mashed potatoes with some other vegetables.

When they got home from work, they asked how I got in and I told them. They seemed to be pleased to see me. We ate supper and I ducked all questions except to say that things were never going to work out for me out there with Karyn, so I decided to come home. I asked if I could stay home until I got back on my feet again and that I would pay them for my board.

They agreed and I had a feeling of being safe. The next day I filed for unemployment insurance.

Around Christmas sometime I was washing the dishes at the house and my mother was drying them. The questions about what had happened out west were relentless. I just did not respond. I did not know what to tell her. Did I want her to know I was a complete fool? I just did not reply. But then the questions started about the baby. I could not take it any longer and I just broke down. With tears streaming down my face I turned and yelled at her to leave me alone. And I ran upstairs. I lay crying on my pillow reflecting that out there was going to be a little girl that now had to grow up without her father. My mother never asked me again about this nightmare that I had just been through.

Over these past years I had tried marijuana and hash. I was careful when using it, because I always had to keep my wits about me, and I could only depend on me. My understanding of everything that was going on was already blurred normally. Unlike booze, this drug let me relax and be calm and I was able to suppress my guilt and emotions to some extent. It seemed that nearly everyone was smoking the stuff. It only took a couple of tokes in the right environment for me to be relaxed and in full laughing mode at most everything. I felt great to be able to let my guard down for the first time in my life and have the most belly laughs, mostly at myself. Smoking this stuff with my friends at times gave me the ability to look at myself and the others in the room and to know that they had to be feeling the same silly way as I did. For the first time in my life I felt that I was not inferior, just different.

I noticed that some friends were smoking marijuana nearly every day, and that concerned me. Some, including my brother, were using other stuff as well, LSD for example, which I never would touch. I saw addiction happening before my eyes with some people and I knew I was not going down that road. I knew I liked the sensation that pot gave me, and it seemed to help me when feeling depressed. I would only take a puff or two once in a while. I was afraid of it, mostly because I liked it, and I knew I had to depend on me in this world, not on a drug.

I also went to visit Charlie Campbell, the older British pigeon racing friend of mine that always kept my pigeons for me in his loft when I left home. It was a very good day as I remember. I helped him clean his loft and we handled and talked about each bird. He explained what he had been doing with my birds and his while I was gone. He kept my line breeding program method recorded and up to date. He raced my birds with his and told me how each one had flown and showed the race result sheets to me. We then decided that this upcoming racing season we would fly both his and my birds as partners. I was tickled pink to get back in the game. I was at his loft every chance I got.

CHAPTER

10

New Beginnings

O f course, now back at home, the search was on for work again. I spoke to the city about working at one of their rinks, making ice and taking care of the chalet as I had done other years for winter work. But, of course, they already had their people in place for that winter. I was collecting my unemployment check every two weeks and this got me through the winter. With odd jobs here and there.

I often dug out my suit and tie and worked hard trying to get interviews for a full-time job. I thought I would be a good salesman of a quality product that I believed in and fully understood. Yet each time I ran into the same problems. I spoke very little French and I could not understand stuff written on paper. I had good verbal skills and I looked clean cut, but I was bleeding to death inside every time the answer was sorry, you do not qualify. No matter how hard I tried to understand, why would my brain not let me read and write very well like others? I was always told I was as smart as anyone else, I just needed to apply myself. I knocked on a lot of doors looking for that one person who could see that I was going to be one of the very best employees that they had. I was willing to do anything and to work harder and longer than anyone else. It was tough to keep mentally sound with each rejection though.

At this time, I reconnected with a childhood friend of mine Claude. He liked and kept pigeons in his backyard and joined the racing club as a junior member as well. We use to do a lot of fishing together at the river. He was a year older and we hung out together at times.

Years later I helped him land a job at the huge printing plant in the east end of Montreal where I worked sweeping floors and running errands for all the pressmen. Being French, Claude got to work on the printing presses as an apprentice pressman's helper ahead of me because it was a French shop, I was told by the foreman.

Claude had married Pat who I knew to be a very nice girl. They had a daughter Paula and were living in St. Lambert. One day Claude and I met up and I asked if he wanted to go ice fishing on Lake Champlain with me. We did not have any ice fishing rigging so we made some. We got hold of an old umbrella and took off all the ribs in it. Each rib formed a hinged T. At one end of the T we wrapped the line and the other end we fixed a lead weight. The center of the rib we stuck at the side of the fishing hole in the ice. So with a fish on the line, it would pull that end of the T down and the other end would go up letting us know we had a fish on the line.

The next weekend we went to the lake to ice fish. We took my car that day. Right beside the lake there was a variety store that sold bait and we bought some bait minnows to put on the many lines that we were going to use. Most fishermen drove onto the lake right beside the store. There was a fairly steep grade driving down onto the ice. That was not a problem getting off the ice if you built up enough momentum.

We spent the whole day way out on the ice. Claude smoked cigarettes and by midday he was out of them and asked me to drive over to the store and get him a pack, and I did. When I got within fifty yards of the bank I knew I had to accelerate to get up it. I noticed that there was a windswept area about sixty feet wide across my route, looking like an open space of water. It got my attention for a split second before seeing that it was clear but solid ice. I went back to Claude and gave him his smokes and we continued to catch a good number of fish keeping fairly busy tending about ten lines.

Later on it started to lightly snow and it was getting dusk. So we called it a day, picked up all our gear and fish and loaded the car. Once we started back we could no longer see the store because the snow was a little heavier and it was a little dark. I just followed the trail of tire marks back to shore. Knowing I had to accelerate to make it up the upcoming bank, I did and was going all of forty miles an hour I heard a loud four-letter word, the passenger door flew open and Claude was gone. I looked back in my mirror and there was Claude going ass over tea kettle, arms and legs all over the place sliding behind me on the ice. I did not stop as I was at the grade at the bank. I got out of the car to see if he was alright. He was now upright and trying to find his toque in the snow. Once he got to the top of the bank, looking like a car wreck himself, I asked laughing, what the hell were you trying to do. He said I thought you were driving into open water and I bailed. I was laughing so hard and I said, Nice Guy, you bailed out and didn't even care to warn me! I have cracked up many times thinking about that fishing episode.

I had the privilege and honour of becoming godfather for Pat and Claude's new baby son Paul. Proud that he carries my name Paul Ian DesRuisseaux.

I had the privilege and honour of becoming godfather for my friend Claude and his wife Pat's new baby. I am proud that he carries my name Paul Ian DesRuisseaux.

Patsy holding Paul after Christening with me on the right.

IAN COBB

Most of the St. Lambert fellows that I knew then had jobs and cars and were doing well for themselves. Some still lived at home but some had their own apartments now. We often went to watch the Expos baseball games and Montreal Canadiens hockey games together. Followed by a night at the clubs having a few pints on the weekends. I always had to budget my spending so that would be the only reason I did not drink as much as most. I worked again for Clipper Ship Supply that summer and fall.

I ran into my childhood friend Jake Carter again and he mentioned that he had joined the YMCA and the Aquadine Scuba diving club. I joined the club the next week. This was right up my alley. I already had a fair bit of experience with scuba diving but I was never certified. I was always a very good swimmer and I just loved the way John Rogers and others organized and led this very fun diving club. We trained and practised safety every Tuesday night in the pool and went diving most weekends. I never did tell anyone that I could not read or write very well, and somehow I got certified under John's tutelage and patience. I still had some inferiority complexes that I carried before joining Aquadine. But I knew that I was a very good swimmer and without any fear of water, just respect for it, and that I could compete with the best of them. This club changed my whole life in general. I could comfortably dive and belong to the most beautiful group of people I had ever known. I fit right in without having to pretend I was someone else. We all trained, travelled, camped, dove, ate and drank together. We were all brothers and sisters who often were responsible for each other's lives and well-being. We trusted each other. John instilled confidence and safety in all of us as one of our leaders but he really was just one of us. We all had the most beautiful time of our lives together. John was the Vice-President of Molson's Brewery and later on became

Chairman of the board. But you would never know it; with us he was just one of the guys.

When my wife Dawn and I left Montreal to build our new life and eventually my ranch in New Brunswick. I asked John many things and he always gave me encouragement and positive feedback. He, his wife Maureen and daughter Kacey and other divers spent time in N.B. on my ranch, every time heading to different dive sites in the Maritimes. I was very proud to have John as a friend. I once introduced him to someone as the V.P. of Molson's; a short time after the introduction, John called me aside and told me sternly to never again introduce him that way. I felt very badly at the time, but I had just learned a very important lesson that I always carry with me today. "Humility".

When I first started building my fur farm in N.B. without any money and I could not borrow any, I remember wondering if I was going to make it as a first generation farmer in the fur farming business and asked for some of John's advice about a few things. His words to me were, "Ian, this country was built by people like you, you are doing great. Believe in yourself and persevere." His words and his friendship are one of the main reasons that I worked harder and eventually built two of the most productive fur operations in the1970's and 80's without borrowing.

We trained every Tuesday night at the Y and we dove nearly every weekend as a group everywhere around the area. Rivers, lakes and quarries. On long weekends we would drive to the State of Maine or Massachusetts to dive. We would dive on shipwrecks. We always camped with tents and brought our Coleman stoves and Bar-B-Qs. In winter we would cut two holes in the ice a far distance from each other, and using our compasses would navigate under the ice from one to the other. We always trained and practiced safety at all times and used the buddy line system.

Once nine of us worked all one morning cutting a large chunk of ice from the shore of the St. Lawrence River. With our fins kicking and our hands pushing this ice, we floated it out into the current of the river and then we all hopped on board. It was a warm spring day and we were all very warm wearing our dive suites. Our cooler was in the middle of our ice raft, along with a couple of wooden benches and a flag that we had stuck into the ice. We had a great ride down the river for about two hours or so. When the cooler was empty, we got back in the water and pushed our ice raft to shore, where two other club members, who were following along on the road, picked us up with their vans.

I was now spending all of my time working or with my pigeons, going to the Expos baseball games, Montreal Canadiens hockey games, the YMCA and scuba diving. Things were going fairly well except for not having a good steady job.

After my pipeline transmission construction career ended, I did a lot of scuba diving in different oceans and fresh waters around the globe. Some of the most fantastic times of my life! I spent many hours viewing the underwater life of many creatures. In caves, on the bottom and on reefs. There were new discoveries and observations for me on every dive. Sports diving with great people helped me get my self-confidence back again.

I was still looking for a decent full-time job when another former friend, Mike Holmes who also went pipelining with us, had just started working for The Montreal Gazette newspaper as a circulation district manager, told me they needed another district manager. So It was time again to dig out the suit and get in for an interview. This time I came up with a different wrinkle for my application and interview for this position. Mike had told me all about what criteria they were looking for. After rubbing a little black shoe polish on my right hand and wrist, looking like a very bad bruise and putting my arm in a sling, I showed up for my interview at the newspaper personnel department.

Before my interview I asked the very obliging secretary if she could help me fill out my application form because I had just taken a fall and injured my hand. I had her write four years at McGill University for education. I knew it was a well respected school and it sounded good. Even though I could not even spell the name. I got the job.

This job did not pay like work on the pipeline did, but it was enough to get my own apartment in St. Lambert and buy a small Toyota truck to deliver the bundles of newspapers to all my newspaper boys and all the stores that I delivered to. I now had a full-time job with a respectable company. Mike also helped me understand my job requirements. I enjoyed my work thoroughly, working as hard as I could at doing it well.

One Saturday night after a Boston versus Montreal Canadiens hockey game that we won by the way, my four or five friends and I headed just across the street from the Forum to The Father's Mustache dance club to celebrate as we always did. It was a large place, with a dance floor and band stage and always packed with young people. By the time we got into the club after a game, all the tables were always full. So we all used to order our beer sitting or just standing at the bar. It was a good spot because everyone coming or going would have to pass by. Perfect for checking out the ladies. That night we noticed three or four girls sitting at a table together and I was looking for someone to dance with. I asked one of them for a dance and we danced a few. I found out they were all working at the Montreal Children's Hospital one street over. And three of them lived together in an apartment one block away.

I think it was the next Saturday night that I spotted the same gal again with two or three friends. And again I had a few dances with all of them. It was a fun night. When leaving I asked if I might walk them the short distance home, and so I did. I was invited up to their apartment for a coffee and I said sure. I found out all three had lived and trained in New Brunswick. As I left I asked for a phone number from this particular girl, whose name was Dawn, and I put it in my wallet.

It was about two or three weeks before Christmas and our diving club was having a Christmas swim party and dance at the Y. Most of the other club members were taking girlfriends and wives to this event, but I did not have a date. I thought about inviting Dawn and I thought I would give her a call to see if she was available to go with me. I called her and she was going to think about it. I called back a couple days later and she said she would go. On the night of the party, I picked her up at her apartment and went to the YMCA. We had a great time. Dawn met and liked all the dive club gang and she joined in different outings with all of us.

I thought that her being a hospital worker, that she was well versed on contraceptives. After dating some time, she became pregnant and I was surprised by this. She asked me if I thought she should have an abortion. I agreed that she should. I did not want to bring another child into this world and not be there. And I was just starting to get back on my feet emotionally after the fiasco with Karyn out west. After the procedure, we dated close to a year before I gave her a ring and asked her to marry me. Around this time, I told Dawn that I had a daughter out there someplace and what I had been through trying to do the right thing. I told her that once I had money enough, I would someday find her.

We were planning to go to New Brunswick for Christmas, where I would meet her parents. One night I was heading back home to my apartment across the Victoria bridge. It was freezing rain that night. The salt truck had done all of

Bridge street and I had very good traction. The truck had turned around and salted the other side of the road going back. As soon as I went through the old toll gates I was spinning towards a four foot high cement lane divider. There was nothing I could do, except hold on and brace for impact.

I heard in the distance someone softly calling my name and I opened my eyes to see a nice-looking nurse leaning over me wiping my forehead. As I came around many hours later, I saw that I was lying in a hospital room and the nurse told me that I had a car accident and I was in the Montreal General Hospital. The doctor asked questions as they assessed me for damage. I had broken my leg in three places and also needed a fair amount of stitches around my eye and head area, and I had suffered a pretty good concussion. He asked if there was anyone that they could call for me. I told them that my fiancée worked in the x-ray department at the Montreal Children's. Not that far away. I do not remember how long they kept me in the hospital before Dawn took me back to the three girls' apartment, where I stayed and slept on their couch. Cast and all.

Meeting Dawn's parents in New Brunswick with a broken leg.

After a few weeks Dawn and I boarded a train to St. Stephen New Brunswick for Christmas and to meet her folks as we had planned. She was now wearing my engagement ring that she had just accepted from me. We were very happy and excited. But I have to tell you about this train trip to Mcadam N.B. train station where her Dad was to pick us up. What a trip, me on crutches in a cast way past my knee with the two of us in a single sleeper compartment, not a room just a bed and curtain that our seat was turned into by the porter.

The one vivid experience of that trip was me having to squeeze into and sit down on the toilet at the end of our car. I could not bend my leg with the cast on it and the wall was about fifteen inches in front. There was no other way. I had to put the cast leg up the wall and try to sit at the same time. What a mess! Poor Dawn had to help me clean up. I just prayed that I would not have to visit a second time.

Dawn's Dad picked us up and drove a fairly long way to their home. I have to tell you, even with my broken leg, It was by far my best family Christmas ever at their small country home that her father had built years ago. With four siblings home, and a lot of great country cooking. I was very happy to now be a part of such a solid family.

When we arrived back in Montreal I continued to stay at the three girls' apartment on the couch. It was a colonial style, with wooden spindles and not too solid to accommodate my cast and me. I do not remember how long I stayed with them, but I do know that little couch was beat up by my cast pretty good. I must have been out of work for a couple months while still on crutches and I do not remember if I got rid of my apartment or not. I had a pretty good concussion and maybe that is why I cannot remember much about that period. This was my third or fourth concussion, and it took a long time to clear, if it ever did or not, I'm not sure. My long-term memory is very vivid. But I had noticed more and more that my short-term memory was not so good.

We were married that spring in May; we both were working and planning our future. We lived in a nice three-bedroom basement apartment in St. Lambert and slowly furnished it. I was very proud of my wife and I was a very happy man. I loved Dawn and she loved me. I did however carry some guilt for not letting her know that I was somewhat defective goods, but then again, I didn't even understand myself why I had so much trouble trying to cope with different things. Shame always kept me from telling anyone.

Our wedding day, surrounded by diving buddies with whom we had many wonderful times.

The two years before we were married and the next three were by far and away the very best five years of my life. Dawn and I had fantastic times camping and partying with mostly the diving crowd. On most of our dive trips we all sat around bonfires telling stories, having a few pints or just looking at the stars. And, of course, being in the water searching for treasure, watching and studying the diverse marine life or entering caves on the seafloor was euphoria for me. I was in my natural environment of total tranquility and exploration. Dawn could not swim but she had Keith who was a dive club member and the aquatics director for the Y teach her. At least now she was drown-proof. With us being on the water so much it was a little more comfortable for me. I was very proud of her effort as she was timid of the water. She even practised a little wearing a mask and snorkel. On one occasion in the Caribbean we dressed Dawn in some neoprene, a life jacket, mask, fins, and snorkel. We then towed her out over the coral reef that we were all diving on. The visibility was as clear as glass from the surface down to the bottom thirty or forty feet where we were diving. She now had a glimpse of the fantastic underwater world of colours and marine life on these reefs that I talked about.

Feeding a sea urchin to a smaller reef fish. Diving introduced me to a magical undersea world of discovery.

I have hundreds of stories of my underwater adventures that I could tell you. Here are a few.

One dive on a beautiful reef in the Caribbean, my buddy that day was Jake. We were just cruising along near the sand bottom on the open ocean side of a reef taking in the sights and marine life about forty feet down on my depth gauge. I happened to see a small gap between the seafloor and the coral reef. I went to investigate. There are often different species of fish or turtles that hide under these type of crevices and I thought I would check it out. When I stuck my head under the reef peering in, I notice it widened and looked like a small cave opening. I went in about the length of my body and saw that it seemed to continue further. So I went back out to motion Jake to follow me. He and I squeezed under and sure enough it opened up so that we both could kneel and give each other hand signals. This opening went a little to the right and we started to follow it further into the floor of this reef. We continued single file as that was as wide as this opening was. We had travelled further in and to a fair bit to the right, when I notice that there was no longer sand under us but coral.

The light was nearly gone as I tried to read my depth gauge on my arm. It now told me that as we were going in that we were also ascending some. We decided to turn around and head back. Then I noticed that there was a faint glimmer of light coming from further into this cave. Jake and I exchanged hand signals again and decided to press on. We had lots of air left, so we started towards this bit of light, not knowing how far away it was or even if we could get to it. Further in, the narrow passageway opened up into a small room. I was pretty excited but started to get a little concerned that if anything happened to one of us, our tanks or air hose this far in, it was going to be interesting getting back out. I looked at my depth gauge again and showed Jake that we had gone up about fifteen feet but the light was getting brighter.

As we went along we could see that there was a hole of light that we were heading for. As we approached this hole, it started to look like it was going to be too small for us to get through. And if we tried we might hit the valve on the top of our tanks on the hard coral. That would not be very good. Once I got to this hole, I knew I was not going to get through it. I contemplated going all the way back and thought there must be way to enlarge this hole or something. Right away I realized that this coral was way too hard to try breaking off using my dive knife. I then thought of another way. I hand signalled Jake to watch me. Then I took my tank off my back and kept my regulator in my mouth and fitted my tank through the hole bottom end first. I was afraid of my tank falling on the other side of the hole so I very tightly held onto the valve as I started to squeeze my head and shoulders through.

The water was so warm there I would only wear a white T-shirt when diving. Not much protection from scraping against the sharp coral. I made it out with only a few scratches and put my tank back on. Jake, I knew, was going to be able to get out because he was much thinner that this chunky guy. Jake handed me his tank through the hole and followed it out. We had just popped right out of the top of the reef when I felt Jake grab my arm in a way that I knew there was a problem. He pointed behind me and when I turned I saw exactly what the problem was. Motionless, not twenty-five feet away, was the largest barracuda that I have ever seen. And believe me I have witnessed many. Some in schools and some alone. I knew when one of these guys was hunting and that is just what he was doing, stalking us. I knew that my small bleeding cuts and scratches were putting scent particles in the water. Most people fear sharks. But I have to tell you, one of the deadliest fish in the ocean is barracuda. They are just too fast to defend against. More that one diver has had his head taken off instantly by these guys. Your mask looks like a fishing lure from the penetrating sunlight shining on it.

The only thing we had to defend with was our dive knives that we took out of our leg sheaths. We both stood on top of the reef with our knives in front of us looking straight at this big fella lying horizontal. Only his gill fin moved slightly as I looked him right in the eye. He looked about ten feet long. All of a sudden with just one quick shudder he vanished.

It was so quick that we did not know if he went up, down or ahead, even with that clear water. We had no idea which way he went. But as we made our way back to our dive boat, we sure kept our eyes open. It was a great campfire story that Jake and I had to tell that night.

One of our diving trips to Grand Cayman Island, there must have been twelve or fifteen of us. This was one of my favorite group trips ever. We flew to Miami on a 747, the largest plane I had ever been on. Then after a short wait we boarded Cayman Airways to the Island. John had discovered a diver's-only smaller resort there, which we moved into for ten days or so. We all had our own cabin right beside the water's edge and this resort's wharf, where this beautiful dive boat was parked. There was a main dining hall and ping-pong and lounge room.

When we wanted a beer, pop or anything we just took it and marked it down in a book beside our name that was on the counter. I think there were just two other people there and our club members. I use to get out of our cabin in the morning before breakfast and just slide into the sea snorkeling in the vivid clear water. There was always something for me enjoy moving across the bottom or in the water.

The sea was very warm from top to bottom there. We would never need a dive suit in these waters, no thermal climes at any depth. We dove twice a day at many different locations. Once when our dive boat was anchored about three miles offshore, most of us went over the side for a dive.

At one point there were four of us gliding along the bottom and I wondered why we had gone over a certain area a couple of times.

When I suddenly spotted something in front slightly buried in the sand, I brushed a couple of inches of sand away with my hand. And to my surprise I found an old historic clay type wine bottle. I held it up to show the others. It still had a cork in it. After everyone inspected it I put it into my catch bag and we continued our dive. I could hardly wait to get back on board our boat and inspect this treasure further.

Once we were all on board I excitedly told about and showed the rest our find. One of the divers suggested that I should open it so we all might have a taste of wine from the last century. I went to the galley and came back with a corkscrew and eagerly I got the wine bottle opened. But alas only sea water and sand poured out. Then suddenly a piece of wet paper came out as well with the sand. Could this have been tossed into the sea many years ago from some far off place? I was excited as I very carefully opened up this fragile wet paper. On it was written in bold letters, "HI IAN"

My buddies got me again!

This is the old clay wine bottle I keep to remind me of the best years and friends of my life.

A couple days later at breakfast, we asked for a show of hands for how many of us wanted to go on a night dive. I believe there were ten of us. So that night we went to a place called Seven Mile Beach where we entered the water from the shore.

About a quarter mile out in front was a coral reef that had a break in it. Large fish from the open water would pass through this break to hunt and feed on the inside edge of the reef. We all discussed our game plans for any eventuality all that afternoon. I buddied up with Jake. We both had great handheld divers' lights and both of us knew each other's strengths and weaknesses.

Once the beach bonfire beacon was lit, all five pairs of divers headed out in a fan formation. Jake and I wanted to head towards the hole in the reef by going along the bottom using our compasses and lights. I could not believe the volume of illuminated plankton and different microscopic organisms in our light beams through the water. The coral reef and sea floor is much more active and a different place at night. All the sea urchins come down from the coral and spread out over the sea floor at night to feed. These are black urchins with needle sharp five-inch barbed quills.

As Jake and I proceeded along the bottom I spotted a very large turtle sleeping under a piece of brain coral, with his eyes closed. I gave my light to Jake and he pointed both lights at this sleeping turtle, I motioning to him that I was going to put my gloved hands on either side of him so I might control him. I slipped under the piece of coral and grabbed onto both sides of him. Well, I was not quite ready for that burst of power. He took off like a racehorse out of the gate with me hanging on to him. Within five seconds I could no longer see the lights that Jake was holding. Total black and I had to let go.

The first rule of diving is if you lose your buddy, you surface. Once I got to the surface, Jake was already there. I swam over to him took my light and we went back to the bottom. We were not comfortable being "food splashing" on the surface. We spent another thirty minutes watching whatever marine life happened across our light beams. We only saw one shark on that night dive; it was a blue shark and not very big. We surfaced again to get our bearings and distance from our bonfire beacon. We decided to use our fins and swim on the surface back to shore. Very unnerving, swimming on the surface in shark waters, and in the dark I have to tell you. I could feel one hungry shark just behind me as we headed to shore. All five pairs of divers arrived back at the beacon within fifteen minutes of each other or so. We had all experienced similar emotions and I for one decided that one night dive was plenty good enough for me, thank you.

We were always pulling pranks on each other, like the time coming back from Cayman. We had a two-hour or more layover at the Miami airport. We all sat around two tables in the bar right across from the security gate for our flight home on Air Canada. It was a warm day and most of us were having our last vacation brews together. A few of us were drinking beer and tomato juice. You know those small tomato juice cans. Well after we had many beer, they called our flight. So we gathered up our belongings to walk across the hall to go through the metal detectors and into our holding area. I thought I had better make a pit stop at the washroom first. So I headed for the john only a few feet away. I finished and went quickly back to my chair where all my things were. I saw the others across the hall inside the holding area. I grabbed my jacket and all of my things and walked the few feet across the hall and through the metal detectors. Every alarm in the airport seemed to start screaming and the security people came towards me. What was going on? I lifted up my head and looked at all the gang inside waving and laughing at me. I still had no clue until the security guards started emptying my jacket pockets. Yeah, you guessed it. All my cowboy friends had stuffed my pockets and even the side pouches of my bags with empty tomato juice cans. I looked up to see my wife and all the rest having a very fun time at my embarrassment with the custom officers trying to explain.

Some months later Dawn announced to me that she was pregnant and we both were very excited. We started pricing and looking for a house and making plans. A couple of weeks later we were driving home on a very rough and hilly road from a long weekend of diving in Massachusetts with all the gang. The day after we arrived home, Dawn told me she was spotting some blood and she miscarried a couple of days later. She said that it was because of me driving too fast on the rough road back, which I was. We were both disappointed, and I felt very sad and guilty for causing this miscarriage. I really thought I had caused it. It would be a long time before we knew what the real problem was.

We carried on working and having a very good time traveling to different places with our friends, diving and camping. We were having a good life together and planning our future.

I was very busy working as a district manager for The Montreal Gazette and Dawn working for The Children's Hospital. We were starting to save money for the day we would try to buy a house.

I worked for a morning paper and that meant getting up at 3 or 4am to deliver all my bundles of newspapers. I would be back home by 10am for a break, then into the office to do paperwork, phone calling customers and carriers et cetera. I had to collect money from my stores and carriers. Balancing my deposits and filling out forms was always a challenge for me. I would often ask for help from others. The job outside the office was very busy working with my newspaper delivery carriers and a lot of driving over large areas of the city. I liked it and did it well, I thought.

I worked hard and took pride at increasing newspaper sales in my district. I had my carrier boys out canvassing for new customers a lot. The newspaper would supply me with different sports items as prizes for my boys who got the most new customers. I even formed a softball team with a lot of my boys that came out the most to canvass with me. The Gazette was so pleased with the effort we put in and how much we increased newspaper sales for them that they paid for a trip to Disney World in Florida for all the boys, myself and another district manager.

The Gazette

MONTREAL

Mr. Ian Grant Cobb,
District Manager.

Montreal, April 17th, 1973.

Congratulations on the attainment of your quota during the last contest that ended March 31st, 1973. It is refreshing to see that some District Managers will put in the necessary time and efforts to achieve a personal goal under difficult conditions. The quota was set in order to seek out distinction amongst our team of District Managers. You have distinguished yourself during this last contest.

I feel the rewards are certainly forthcoming and I am not necessarily referring to the monetary aspect of the job. However, I do hope that you will enjoy the trip to Florida and that upon your return you will be stimulated to greater accomplishments in your present function.

Again, congratulations.

Gérard S. Séguin,
Director of Newspaper Sales.

GSS:fc

Montreal Gazette Party

A congratulatory letter on a successful sales record would soon be followed by getting fired for lying on my application.

I had a great time with the kids. First, Disney was a blast each day and back at the motel I would make up treasure hunts for them, took them all to Marineland and just kept them busy. They were mostly well behaved kids on the trip. One evening I sat around telling them stories of some of my adventures and experiences with birds and animals. It was a very enjoyable week for me with these kids, some of whom had never even been off the Island of Montreal In their lives before.

After working for the Gazette for two years, I thought I had now proven myself as a quality employee. My office work, however, was not up to standards and I needed to ask for help from others at times.

They soon found out that I could not read or write very well, and that on my application I'd had the personnel department secretary fill out my application. And that I had told her I had just fallen while I was wearing a fictitious sling on my arm. With a little black shoe polish rubbed on my wrist for a bruising appearance. I had her write down that I had two years of McGill University. When I told them that I could not read or write, I was fired for lying on my application.

I tried to take this as professionally as I could. I shook my boss's hand, thanked him for what I had learned and apologized to him for being deceitful. I left chin up, got into my car and cried all the way home to my new wife with another manufactured story to tell her why. I can't remember what I told her other than I had been laid off. This is how I lived, with one lie leading to another.

I finally had had enough of trying to find others to give me work. I made up my mind that I was going into business for myself from now on.

I am not sure where or when that I had met a fella that told me he fire-proofed and cleaned range hoods, ducts, and vents for a large chain of take-out restaurants. I wondered if I could start that kind of a business. So I had some business cards made, got my three-piece suit on

Jan G. Cobb

MANAGER

COBB INDUSTRIAL CLEANERS REG'D.

169 GREEN #1
ST. LAMBERT   TEL. 672-7215

Launching myself as an entrepreneur with a lot of imagination and some deception.

and I start calling on every restaurant that I could find on the streets and in large buildings.

I remember talking to the stationary engineer of some building in Montreal. He asked me if we cleaned ductwork. I said we did lots of them. He told me that a few hundred pounds of grain dust had been sucked into his ductwork by some kind of accident. He asked me for a price and I told him I could only do this job by the hour, because I could not know how difficult this type of dust might be to remove. It was not just regular dust like our other contracts. So I gave him a price per hour and he agreed. I asked my wife Dawn to help me type out a simple price per hour contract for him to sign, because she could type and typing looked more professional than my handwriting.

I already had my small truck that I used for my newspaper job. I just needed a shop vacuum, dust masks and a few more things. I already had a full tool box. I brought the contract over for him to sign and told him we could fit in this work in a few days. I did the job in five days and was paid. I was now in business for myself.

I was telling one of my long time friends Wil-John about my new business that I had started. Dawn and I were visiting him and his wife who were also our neighbors in St. Lambert. Wil-John always worked with his hands and was a university grad. He restored old furniture for customers. He had even taken down an old historic wooden house and rebuilt it board by board on his small piece of property for his family home. Wil-John and I had been hotel roommates as well on some pipeline jobs. I asked him if he was available to help me with my new business, if I got more work than I could handle myself, and he said he would.

I had an idea a few days before when I was trying to get a duct cleaning job in the tallest building in Montreal. With my suit and tie on, I had a quick meeting with the stationary engineer of the sixty-floor office tower and presented him with my business card. I told him what my company did and I asked if I could bid on the next time the building's ducts needed to be cleaned. He told me that there was nothing in their budget for such work and they never had it done before. He also told me that no other building cleaned their ductwork either. I thanked him and asked him to keep my card.

The next day with my three-piece suit on and business cards in hand I asked and received a meeting with the Fire Chief of the Montreal Fire Department. I explained to him that my company had been looking at this high rise building, and that we had noticed it was prime for a major fire. I also asked the Chief that our meeting be recorded on paper, because I did not want any repercussions to come back on me for not reporting this very serious situation. I explained to him that the ductwork in the whole building was full of flammable dust, it would only take a spark to create a major disaster.

I told this story to him because many years earlier, when I worked in the grain elevators down at the harbour, I was told how flammable dust was and if we were caught smoking around the grain elevators we would be fired on the spot.

A week later I received a call from the office tower building engineer to come in to his office and give him a price to clean their ductwork for the sixty floors. I knew there was no one else doing that work so I priced it by the hour. Unlike today, when we all receive many phone calls from call centres for duct cleaning services.

On the thirtieth floor of this building that we were cleaning was the air conditioning system for the whole building and the engineer showed me around it one day. It was quite a system. Water would stream over a room full of aluminum coils and fins that a huge fan would blow air through. The now cooler air was then blown through the total building's ductwork cooling the building. But I noticed that all over the fins and coils was a quarter inch thick calcium and mineral deposit.

Over the next couple days I pondered about what I had seen on these fins and coils. I knew that it was the cold aluminum that the air needed to contact for cooling, not a quarter inch build up of mineral deposit. So I called the building engineer on the phone and asked him if he ever had measured the temperature and volume of the air entering the ductwork of the building from the cooling system. He said he had and I told him that I could increase the efficiency of the air condition of his building by increasing the volume of air and decreasing the temperature of the air. I had no idea if my idea was going to work or not but I thought what I had in mind might just work. He said he was very interested and I gave him a heavy fixed price.

I went to the hardware store and purchased a high pressure washer and hand pump sprayer and spoke to the manager of the chemical department about what type of acid might take water mineral deposits off of aluminum without damaging it, He decided on a type of acid that would work for me and I bought a five-gallon pail. Next day I had the building engineer take a temperature and volume reading before I did anything.

I put on my breathing mask and I sprayed the whole room's coils and fins with the acid. After an hour using my

500 psi high water pressure washer, I blasted all the deposit off of every piece of aluminum in the room. All of this deposit fell off onto the catch basins that were at the bottom of all the aluminum structures. The mineral crust was now over a foot deep in these basins. The aluminum now dazzled sparkling clean as a whistle. Even I was impressed.

I was now anxious for the engineer to take another reading of air flow and air temperature. He reported his findings back to me a day or two later, and told me it had improved substantially. So now I had another service to sell. I worked hard trying to get more contracts, but I was only getting enough work to get by on, along with my wife's income. With Dawn and I both working we were doing okay.

We now had saved about $8000 in our bank account. And no debt. My brother was married and he and his wife found a house in St. Lambert that they wanted to buy. But he did not have the down payment for it, and asked me. After we worked out an interest rate that was more than the bank paid and a monthly repayment amount, I loaned him most of what Dawn and I had saved.

We were wanting to start a family and once we had a baby to care for, Dawn would have to leave her job and I was not doing well enough in business to be able to carry the day. So we decided that once she was pregnant, we were going to move out of Quebec. I was thinking of bringing up my family in the Okanagan Valley in B.C. I might be able to start a farm someplace. But instead we headed to New Brunswick. After all we would have cousins for our kids and other family there.

Our bridesmaid Linda, who was one of the two girls living together with Dawn in Montreal, was now married to Terry and they were living in Riverview and working in Moncton. We called them and told them our plan to move there. They offered us their basement to stay in for a bit until we found a place to live.

CHAPTER
11
Goodbye Quebec
Hello New Brunswick

The day came to prepare to leave. Dawn was well along into her pregnancy. We started packing up the apartment. We paid for the apartment for the next month and I gave the apartment key to a moving company that I had worked for a couple times over the years. I told them that when I found a place to live, I would have them bring our belongings.

Goodbye, Quebec. Hello, New Brunswick.

Moving day finally arrived around June of 1975. With the apartment all packed I dropped the key off at the movers as we drove out of town towards St. Stephen N.B. to visit with Dawn's folks before proceeding to our friends in Riverview near Moncton.

We arrived at Dawn's parents, and I spent some time talking to her Dad about our plans and asked for some advice about what opportunities might be available for us in New Brunswick.

After staying a few days there we headed to Moncton. A place that I knew was the hub of the Maritimes. Situated on the Trans-Canada Highway. They had lots of warehousing, trucking companies, a large railway yard and a diverse economy. There was a large French-Acadian population but unlike in Quebec they all spoke English. Housing was not nearly as expensive as most other places in the country. Surely we should be able to make a life for our family there.

We took the first exit off of the highway, where the sign said four miles to Salisbury and fifteen miles to Moncton. About three miles down this Salisbury road I spotted an old house for sale and asked Dawn if we should stop and ask the people living there how much they were selling it for. Just to have an idea of what country property was selling for, ten miles out of Moncton. The place had a circular gravel driveway and we pulled in. We both got out of the car and I knocked on the door. The couple who owned and lived there answered. I told them why we had pulled into their yard. They could see that Dawn was very pregnant and it was a very hot summer day. They asked us in and offered us both a drink of water. I have to tell you that I have drunk water all over this country. And this water tasted the best and freshest that I had ever drunk. The four of us sat around their kitchen table and just chatted about our and their plans. This fellow said they had recently purchased a store with an apartment upstairs in a community about seventy miles away and were trying to sell this place for some time.

I asked to look around and the fellow showed me around the house while both the gals sat talking. I asked how much land he had here and if I could look around outside. He said there was about eight acres and to just go ahead and look around. He also said that the land went down back all the way to the river. I wondered what river that might be. I had not noticed any water as we drove down this road. I presumed it was a small creek or something like that.

I went out the back door and saw that the alder bush and other trees started about fifty feet from the back of the house. I decided to start working my way through the bush to get a feel for the property. After a while tramping slightly downhill through the bush, I came to some kind of a gully running across the property all grown over with alder. I supposed that this must be the dried creek he was talking about. I went across this gully and through a bit more bush until I did arrive at a good size river. It looked to be three or four feet deep and wider than I could throw a stone across with a good arm. It had good flow with a gravel and stone bottom and was very clear. I thought to myself that this place so far had some promise, as my mind worked at what I could develop this property into if I were to own it.

As I turned from the river and took my first step back to the house, there was a splash near the edge of the river. I looked when it startled me and saw that it was a good-sized salmon. I looked around for more of them for a moment and headed back to the house. I came in the back door. The couple and Dawn were sitting at the table and I asked for another glass of water. I had worked up a bit of a sweat on my walk to the river and back. Again I thought that this was great water and I mentioned it to them. Oh, they said, we have an artesian well here that we are on. Our well water runs out the top all the time all year. It is pure spring water. Wow! I said to myself, that's another plus for this place. All the while I am visualizing how I might build a farm on the piece of ground.

The house itself was tired and needed a lot of work. There were only two screens that I had seen in the basement and the storm windows were still on the house with a lot of flies in between. The basement walls were made of fieldstone a hundred years earlier. The outside walls were clapboard that had been covered years ago with slate tiles. The place needed a lot of work for the person who bought it. We talked a few more minutes before I asked the owner how much money was he asking for the place. I was surprised with his answer when he said $25,000. About a minute later I said that I would give him $22,000. He came back with $23,000. I said that my final offer was $22,500.

I told him that I was going into town to stay with friends. I wanted until this weekend to discuss things over with them and my wife. I asked for a signed paper for the amount we agreed. I took out $50 from my wallet and told him if I was not back by the weekend, in five days, to close the deal, he could keep the $50. He agreed and we left for Linda and Terry's in Riverview, a bedroom community across from Moncton.

We spent the next few days driving all over Moncton and area trying to find something that would work for us for housing and a piece of land as well. After looking at tons of places, from apartments to houses, I turned and said to Dawn, let's go back out to the place we looked at just outside of Salisbury. I think if we can get it, I could build something slowly on that place and get a job in Moncton.

So the next day we drove out to talk again to the home owners. I asked him if he had a mortgage on it and he said he did, at the small village CIBC bank. I said that I would like to take over his mortgage with the bank and we should go to the bank now and have a chat with the manager.

The only collateral that I had to give the bank manager was two years of monthly checks from my brother from the money that I had loaned him. The house owner was already late with his payments because he was also paying another mortgage for his new store that he purchased.

Once I knew that, I put it to the bank manager that we could all come out of this unscathed if we put a deal together. I told the manager that no one else was going to buy this place. That they had been trying to sell for a long time now. I cannot remember how much cash down I gave the bank. It was not very much. Maybe $1000. I had asked my moving company how much they were charging me to deliver our possessions to Salisbury. I kept $600 for the movers and that left Dawn and me about $300 if I remember correctly.

The now former owners had agreed to be out in a week. They already had their new place to move into and had family around that was going to help them.

With Dawn due shortly, I had to put this deal together fast and somehow I was able to get it done.

I called the moving company in St. Lambert and told them to bring our furniture and things right away. We were still staying at Linda and Terry's. The movers arrived the following week. I was very ticked off at the driver that would not drive the moving van onto our new property until I paid him $600 cash which I had planned on doing. Oh well, I guess you can't blame them. There are a lot of people who work at ripping people off. And besides, they were pretty good at unloading and putting everything where Dawn and I wanted things. It took about a week of hard work to get things up and running in our first home. Even being pregnant Dawn worked right along.

We were not in the house more than two or three days when Lillian, our new neighbour, came to the house. She lived across the road from us, up a very long driveway and across a set of railway tracks. In her hands were bags

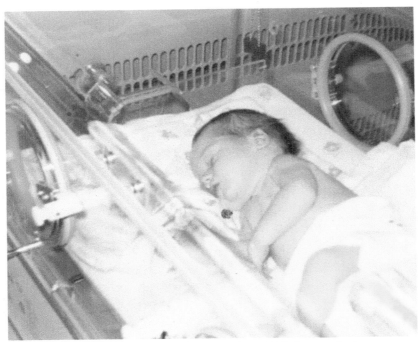

Jeffrey was born premature and had to gain weight before coming home.

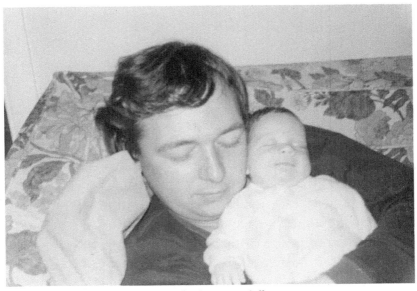

With my firstborn son, Jeffrey.

IAN COBB

full of fresh produce from her garden. Welcome to the neighbourhood, she said. She sat down at our kitchen table that I had just put together and started to chat with Dawn. Lil was a very friendly and pleasant person to be sure. She had one daughter about twelve years old and her husband Paul. When Lillian left, I told Dawn that I knew we were going to make it around here with friendly people like this for neighbours.

It took us some weeks to get the house liveable for us. All the while my head was flashing with different ideas of what I was going to do now for money and how I was going to use this piece of land to be productive for us. Dawn went through the want ads in the Moncton paper and I would phone them asking the requirements of the different jobs.

We spotted an ad for a home improvement department manager with experience at Woolco, in the new and "largest mall east of Montreal," the advertising slogan for The Champlain Mall.

Two months after moving and setting up our first home, Dawn gave birth to our first child, Jeffrey. He was a premature baby and had to stay in an incubator in hospital for a few weeks. It was August 25,1975. No time to fool around now. I needed a job like yesterday!

I lied about my education and retail experience to get the job. I was given a salary plus commission paycheck. So I was motivated to sell as much as I could. I held an introduction meeting with my staff that had been hired months earlier in the set-up phase for this new store. I told them that they were already familiar with the layout and products in the department more than I was and we were going to run this home improvement department as a team. We were all here to promote, sell, order and display product. With good customer service at every turn. I found out in a hurry that Maritimers are very nice people and good workers.

We would all decide on a number of how many units of each product to have on the floor to sell at all times. That would depend on how many units were selling each week and we would add a few more so as never to be out of stock. We did this for every item and piece of plywood and paneling in our department. So if we turned over ten a week, we would order twelve, also depending on how many units were still on the floor when we did the order. I gave everyone a section of the floor to be responsible for in the weekly order book.

After a few weeks of delegating all the operations for running the department to my staff, I was then able to turn my attention to purchasing tractor trailer loads of lumber for the construction contractors. To promote and sell in the outdoor gated bullpen, we had a forklift. Don't forget I was on commission. This was a bit foreign to this retailer, but I told them I had all kinds of experience working retail in western Canada. And the store manager wanted volume sales first and profit second. That worked for me. I called all over to different lumber mills for prices of lifts of 2x4s. All the mills in New Brunswick were owned by K.C. Irving; he also owned half of the province. A well known multi-billionaire. It sure looked to me that he had the total market here and the price was pretty much the same everywhere.

I started to make some calls to lumber mills in Quebec and I quickly came up with a killer price difference. I think the price in N.B. that we were paying was about a dollar per stick of 2x4. But from Quebec I paid 60 cents a stick delivered and sold it for 75 cents. When that hit the newspapers, every Saturday I sold two and sometimes three tractor truck loads of just 2x4s. After a few months I tried to do the same with other products as well. We now had the top sales across Canada by twice. In dollars, not profit. I am getting ahead of myself here.

IAN COBB

In my spare time starting in the spring of 1976, I went to work with a Swede axe cutting down all the bush and trees on my soon to be farm field. For those who might not know what a Swede axe is, it is a U shape bracket with a sharp blade across, on a regular axe handle. That is all I had to knock down the bush behind the house. I had only white cotton gardener's gloves to wear while I slaved away at the bush with the axe. My hands bled right through these gloves everyday. I used alum to numb the pain and thicken the skin. But I kept at it.

After months of hard work cutting down the bush, I spotted in the countryside an old rusted caterpillar D6 bulldozer. I knocked on the house door and asked the fella living there if his dozer was in working order. He said it was the last time he used it. I asked him how much money he would need for me to borrow it. Once he knew that I was new to the area and I was going to start a farm, he offered to bring it over to my place and help me out if I would pay for the fuel and oil. I was thrilled. He ran the dozer when he had time and I ran it as well at times. We pushed all the bush and trees into the gully that ran across the property and leveled the land. We also carved out a pond down back when we noticed two springs that were surfacing there. I was on my way to having a farm.

I had a lot of work inside the house to do as well. But I must confess. The first thing that I built was my pigeon coop. As soon as it was ready I drove to my friend's loft back in Quebec and picked up all my birds from Charlie's loft and brought them home. It was only the youngsters born in New Brunswick that I could let out to fly. The parents had to be kept confined to the fly pen. If they got out, they would fly back to Charlie's loft.

The house we lived in was poorly insulated with old newspapers, and the cold came streaming through the walls and around windows for two winters until we could

First home 1975. Salisbury Road on the Petitcodiac River,
ten miles upstream from Moncton

afford to blow insulation into every cavity in the whole house. The house was heated by a forced air combination furnace, wood and oil. So I scrounged every piece of wood that I could find in the area and lugged it home every time I came across any, so as not to have to buy oil. Sometimes before winter each year I managed to pile two or three cords of dry wood, which cut our heating bill big time.

In 1976, being the friendly guy that I am, I offered my home to have our Woolco store employees' Christmas party. Most of my fellow workers showed up and were having a good time dancing and enjoying the evening when I received a phone call from my neighbours across the way, Paul and Lillian. In fun they told me that they were having a party as well and if I did not come over for a drink, they were all coming over to my place and would drink all of our booze.

I then told Dawn that I was going over to Paul and Lil's place for a quick drink and I'd be back shortly. Three others said they wanted to go over there with me as well. So four of us put on our coats and boots and headed up their long driveway. We wished everyone a Merry Christmas and had a drink. We were just about ready to start back to my place when the phone rang. It was Dawn telling me that I needed to get back right away. Apparently the store manager's wife was one of those who had come across with us. Dawn told me that Bob, our store manager, was drunk and was looking for her and was acting a little crazy. So I told this to my neighbours and we left.

Paul who was a huge man and one of his friends said they wanted to come to my place for a drink and the six of us walked back to the house. Bob went nuts at his wife and a few people got between them so nothing physical would happen. Everyone got back to dancing and were having a good time until Bob hit his wife, knocking her down in my house. Big Paul was the first person to grab him, and he threw him right out my front door and onto the driveway. I told him to go home and not to come back into my house. He pointed at me and hollered something. The personnel manager, Mrs. Gill, told me not to worry as she had seen this performance from him before.

Bob's wife did not want to go home and asked if we would let her stay the night. Dawn and I said no problem with that and I would take her home in the morning. And that is what happened. I told his wife when I dropped her off at her home to at least make a report to the police and I would give a statement also if they wanted me to. The RCMP asked me for a statement and I gave them one. Needless to say, the tension at the store was not very good and Bob was causing some trouble for me.

Mrs. Gill and I had a few talks over the next short while about him trying to create problems for me. So she said that it might be best if I moved to the furniture and appliance department and work on commission there. She said I was a good salesman and would make more money on commission there. So I took her advice and did just that. She was correct; I did make a lot more money in those departments and with no managerial responsibilities.

Building a family, building a ranch

With every spare moment I worked around home, I did not have a barn yet, but I did have my pigeon coop built up on cement posts. Underneath my coop I built three rows of nest boxes for laying hens and ordered a hundred chicks from the hatchery. When the chicks arrived, I put them in a pen that I had made for them in the basement of the house for a few months until they were old enough to transfer outside and under the coop. It did not take too long before I posted a sign at the road for fresh brown eggs. People would bring me all their empty egg boxes and we would fill them every day. I also got some large glass jars and started to sell pickled eggs to the Legions and stores in the area. The only expense was for vinegar, garlic and onion. A lot of work for Dawn and me, to hard-

We raised our chicks in our basement until I was able to build a barn.

Jeffrey holding one of our egg laying hens.

My Dad's first visit in front of my fox ranch sign, with my new barn in the background.

boil and peel all those eggs and pour the hot vinegar on top of them in the jars.

The chickens were free range, saving a lot on feed. But I did go to the Moncton train hump yard often, where all the grain cars were being assembled to send back out west to the grain elevators after dumping off grain into ships at Halifax and St. John ports for export. A hump yard is essentially a large hill, or hump, in the train yard where a locomotive pushes train cars up the hump allowing them to go down the other side of the hill with gravity. At the bottom of the hill a yard man sends the cars onto various tracks to make up different trains as they hit the front coupling on the car to lock the cars together. It is in this hump yard where I would sweep out the residue grain. Mostly barley corn and wheat that was left between the wooden paneling on the box car walls and the metal side of each car. At times I would come home with a 1000 pounds or more in bags on my truck.

Around this time I made an application for a very low interest loan from the New Brunswick Agriculture Department's Farm Adjustment Board. I explained to them my plan to build a silver fox fur farm and they bought into my idea. So they bought out my small mortgage at the bank and I was left with enough money to build my barn. A two storey 50-ft. long by 30-ft. wide insulated steel building on a three-foot concrete wall and floor.

It was now time to resign from my job at Woolco, and I did. I still had the remaining monthly checks from my brother's loan. I would be able to collect unemployment insurance for nearly a year and Dawn wanted to go to work at the hospital and nursing home. She had always told me that she was not interested in being a farmer's wife. So when she went back to work I took Jeffery every place with me. I worked away at whatever I was doing that day, changing diapers and feeding Jeff and always made sure he was safe. We drove everywhere in the truck together. Many times neighbour Lillian would take him for the day if I could not. Even Lil's daughter helped me out babysitting.

One real handicap for me was that Dawn would not go and get a driver's license. She was very scared to drive. I had to take her to work and pick her up about eight miles away every day. I did the grocery shopping and most of the cooking also. It was not until I got angry with her and I would no longer pick up cigarettes and other things for her that she did finally start to learn how to drive with the help of another neighbour. This was the first crack in our relationship.

I was building a ranch no matter what her family thought. I do remember one time Dawn's father talking to me in my barn one day when they came for a visit and knowing we were struggling with dollars. He asked me why I did not go and get a job like everyone else had to do. I told him that we were going to make it my way. I bought Dawn a car once she had her license, and I used the old truck.

I ordered three hundred meat king chicken chicks. The first couple of years I had to keep the new chicks in our basement because I did not have a barn yet. My plan was to grow them to ten or twelve pounds. That you could never find in the store. I killed them and plucked all the feathers and I had all the neighbours over to help clean them in the barn. I paid the neighbours with chicken and sold the rest within the day in the area. Every year after that, I had them all pre-sold and I ordered a couple of times a year for new chicks to grow into roasters. I started taking them to the processing plant for custom kill and dressed which was very cheap and they were packed with ice chips. At a dollar a pound back then, I cleared over $3000 each time that I grew a flock. And don't forget I never had to buy feed. I got all the feed I needed from sweeping out grain cars, and they ranged over the whole field eating everything. So I now had eggs from my hens to sell by the dozen or to pickle, plus the chicken from the meat kings to sell or eat. Every cent went to pay off my load at the Farm Adjustment Board. The eight-year loan was paid off in two and a half years. We were now living debt free again, and that is the way I have lived ever since and always will.

I found a fellow who was logging a few miles away. He was cutting mainly spruce for pulp and paper. But he also had a large pile of cedar that he'd accumulated over time while cutting spruce. I asked him how much he needed for the whole pile of cedar that were in 16-foot lengths. He did not have a market for them and I needed fence poles to surround my soon to be fox ranch. We came to an agreement and he delivered the whole pile to my place. I peeled off all the bark, and now I had poles to surround my whole field with a 12-foot high guard fence. A neighbour farmer brought his tractor and post hole digger over to my field and for a couple of beer and some roasting chickens and eggs he drilled all the holes for my cedar poles. I had to put them four feet down to be below the frost line, leaving twelve feet above ground. Now these were big and heavy poles and I was going to need some help putting them in.

So on the next Saturday I went to the village to look for some help. There were only a couple of businesses there and one was a small diner. It had a coin operated pinball game that the young guys played and hung around at times. None of these kids knew me but I went in to this diner and announced to four or five of them that I was looking for a hand on my farm. They all looked at me as if I was from Mars or somewhere, and I left. I got into my old half ton truck and was about to leave when this young guy came out with a great big smile on his face. He hopped in my truck and said, let's go, what do you need help with? His name was Randy. I told him that I was building a fur farm and I did not have much money with which to pay him, but I would give him what I could. On the way home we picked up a friend of Randy's and we all went to work building my perimeter guard fence. In about a week we had all the poles in the ground and had attached two-inch square light gauge wire to a height of twelve feet.

One day I saw the train track repair crews working and replacing the railway ties on the railway bed across the road near Paul and Lillian's home. I went up to the crossing and saw a lot of discarded railroad ties all along the side of the railway bed. These old creosote ties were going to make the perfect foundation on which to build my furring sheds. I was going to need hundreds of them. I asked one of the railway workers how far they expected to be going on this railway line replacing some of them as they went along. He told me they had a couple of hundred miles on this line to do.

I went home and got my truck and then I grabbed onto the end of the first old railway tie. I was not ready for that kind of weight. These ties were made out of hardwood and were waterlogged. I slowly dragged it to the tailgate of my truck which I had left at the crossing and struggled to lift it onto my tailgate. I could not push it into the box of my truck. So I managed to maneuver the end on the ground into place against the track and then I backed up my truck so the tie was forced into the box. Now this job was going to take a lot of muscle and time, if I was going to drag a couple of hundred ties along the tracks to each closest crossing. I only took three home before I went looking for help. I found Randy and one of his friends to help me. Off and on when I had time, over the next three weeks we had enough railway ties laid out in lines across my field which I could nail the legs of my furring sheds to. It was a very dirty and heavy job to be sure. But the hard work gave me a great foundation to build onto.

All the farmers in the area used a great deal of wire for all types of farming and I saw that the prices were very high in Moncton when I went to price wire. Being from Montreal and having picked up loads of wire and steel at wholesale prices for a ship chandler business, I knew I could do about 50% better in price. So I advertised that I was picking up a load of steel and different types of wire for a very low price if any other farmers wanted in on a great deal. I had so many orders that one farmer supplied his three-ton truck, another paid for the gas and I was able to get all my wire and steel for no cost to me at all. Steel for my barn, wire for my guard fencing, wire for my whole ranch as I built it. I made more than one run to Montreal over the years for different materials needed by me and a large group of farmers including lifts of plywood that I learned where to purchase when I worked for Woolco, at wholesale prices.

I helped an old time fox rancher in the area, part-time for two years during breeding season, with his foxes that he and his father had kept for many years. They were surprised that this city guy knew how to skin, flesh and dry fur. He paid me with already bred female foxes, for my breeding stock.

Back country I also found a small private sawmill operating and I went in to talk to the owner, Mr. Hopper. I told him what I was doing and that I needed lumber to build my operation with. I asked if he needed any help working around his mill or in the woods and said that I could work for payment in board lumber that I needed for my construction. So another great deal was struck.

Twice that year, I had to catch bats that had gotten in the house somehow. One evening Dawn and I were standing at the right side of the house just before dusk and we counted about a hundred bats leaving the gable end of the roof. I had to come up with a plan to stop them coming back into the attic the next morning. The next night I waited for all of them to leave, and then I stapled heavy plastic over every opening along the edge of the shingles where they were coming out from. I thought the problem was taken care of and we slept well. But at sunrise the bats returned, and they woke us up scratching and clawing at our bedroom windows trying to get in. It was crazy. There were hundreds of them covering the side of the house and windows trying to get in. It was creepy for a couple of mornings, and it took a week before they stopped returning.

Once my pond had filled up with water, reaching the overflow gate that I had installed, I stocked it with two hundred trout that I got from the conservation hatchery. I fed them fish pellets and some of my corn and barley that I rolled and cracked up for them. In the spring the river flooded my pond. So really I just stocked the river with most of my trout.

In the winter the pond made a great skating and hockey rink that we all had a good time on for years with friends and neighbours. I had made a small island in the middle and left a tree growing on it. And that is where we put our picnic table in the winter to sit around and put skates on.

The house needed a lot of work inside as well as out. I would pick up materials that were discarded from all over the countryside and find a way to use them. I took out a couple of walls downstairs in the house to open it up and put in a new bathroom and laundry room. We rebuilt four bedrooms upstairs. I put a new roof on and built a very nice front porch, ten feet wide and the whole length of the front of the house. We slowly over the years renovated the house from top to bottom. And I had the most fantastic insulated two-story barn that I could only dream about having years earlier. We had great barn dances upstairs from time to time.

I had another well drilled and I used my artesian well water to heat, air condition and give us all the hot water we needed using the same technology that was being used on the shuttle and space platform. Water was pumped from my artesian well, going through my converter furnace that would extract heat and then the water would exit the home into the other well. It is called a water source heat pump furnace. The total cost to heat, air condition and give us domestic hot water for a year, was only $500 a year. Just the cost of hydro to pump the water from the well to the system was all. I had put the water and hydro underground from the house to the barn when I built it.

Now it was time to start building my fox ranch.

CHAPTER
12
Building a Ranch and a Family

I was ready to move forward. My guard fence was up, I had a road going all the way to the bottom of my field on the left side and I had built a large gate at the bottom of the ranch where I could drive my truck into the ranch area. The first fox pens that I needed to build were my runs to hold about eight to ten female foxes. These pens were 10 ft by 12 ft. and 8 feet high, made out of 2x4 rough lumber with chain link fencing around the whole frame. There were two shelves inside at the back. I put females in these pens in late fall. They needed to be in the open, because they would only start to come into season for breeding with the increase of sunlight.

As their brains receive more sunlight in January, February and March, this triggers a hormone to be released by the brain into their bodies starting them to come into season for breeding. This breeding season starts around January 21st and finishes around March 15th, with most being in season around the 15th of February. Each female only comes into season once a year and only for three days. To maximize fertilization of all her eggs, she needs to be bred late on the second day. The males too, come into and out of season as well. So needless to say I had to be watching and handling all my foxes in the runs from sunup to sundown.

I would always put one male in each run as a teaser to help me see if a female was ready. Then I would read her ID tattoo in her ear and put her with the male that I previously had picked for her to produce the best fur on her pups. These pens I built in my driveway; as I finished each one I would load it crossways across my truck box and take it onto the field, placing them in rows. I had a large picture window upstairs in the barn in a room with a small wood stove and a coffee pot to keep me warm when it was minus 20 degrees. When I was not handling foxes I watched every move on my ranch from that window.

The Ranch in Winter.

One summer day I had just taken a pen down onto the field and when I came back to where I was to start building another I saw a older fella leaning on his small truck with a cigarette in his mouth. I got out of my truck and went over to him. He said you must be Ian, and I said yes. He said I'm Randy's grandfather and I guess I have some time to give you. His name was Arnold Blakeney, he said, as he took a carpenter's tool box out of the back of his truck. I told him I did not have any money to pay him. He said that his time was free of charge. He was well over seventy, and could he ever work. As we worked together I learned that he was a WW2 vet and a master carpenter. He had built half the houses in the village years ago. He was a trapper and he also had a few foxes with one of his four brothers. Arnold had a son, Wayne, who was also a carpenter, and when I had money, I hired him and Randy to help me build.

I homesteaded and built our silver fox ranch in New Brunswick in the 1970s. I built our Mink ranch in PEI in the 1980s. I never borrowed. I bartered, scrounged and worked for all my needs. I live debt free to this very day.

Little by little over years, I built a first-class money-making farm and rebuilt a quality home with part-time help from Randy, Arnold and Wayne. A wonderful family, especially Arnold's wife, Sis, who always had a cup of tea, home baked cookies or a hot meal for anyone who might stop by. She also played grandmother to my kids as well. For all of her and husband Arnold's friendship and help, I had Sears deliver an automatic dishwasher for Christmas. Sis was always doing everyone's dishes by hand for many years. After Christmas, Arnold thanked me in his own way, by saying, now look what you have gone and done, you made another darn job for me to do. I have to build a bigger kitchen counter to accommodate that contraption that you dumped off at my place.

The first couple of years, Arnold helped me skin and pelt my foxes in the basement of our house and my second son Graham stuck to Arnold like glue. Arnold used to call Graham "The Nip Squiggler" and he was just one of these type of men who would give the shirt off his back to everyone. Salt of the earth.

I remember bringing Arnold to the Hudson's Bay Fur Auction in Montreal. He had always trapped fur but had never been to an auction. It was his first time to the big city of Montreal as well. It was a great trip for both of us. And I was very proud to have taken him with me. We toured the huge fur warehouse. It was packed full of every kind of fur in the country from polar bear skins to squirrels. Many millions of dollars worth of fur had been sorted and tagged with the owner's name and number on each pelt. Foxes were being offered for sale that day to buyers from all over the world. Each day after that, other species of fur were scheduled to be sold. All pelts had been sorted and put together, twenty pelts to a ring and hung up for the buyers to inspect days before the auction.

Somehow I had found the time to spend three days in Montreal to visit all the furriers. Knowing the city very well, I went to Mayor Street where the textile and garment manufacturing district was located. I went into many fur garment designers and cutting rooms and spoke to everyone that I could. I introduced myself as one of the finest fur farmers in North America. I believed that I had found a way to artificially inseminate my foxes, and bring more uniformity to their garment industry. And I wanted to know what type of silver fox fur they were most interested in me producing. I wanted to know the length of fur, colour, dark or light silver, density, and texture of coat that would sell for the most money. I told them that I would grow that type of fur for their cutting rooms. It took about ten quality pelts to make one full-length silver fox coat. In the cutting rooms the pelts are cut into stripes about an inch wide and sewn back together into a garment. I would breed my foxes genetically to produce uniformity fur.

And that is what I did. I devised a method to artificially inseminate my breeding females from my best males. I could use one male to breed many females rather than just pairing them up and hoping for the best fur. I believe I was the first person to ever artificially inseminate foxes. It was not easy to find out at what point to inseminate each female to maximize fertilization. But I discovered when and how.

I later sold this method to the zoology industry of North America. After perfecting my system the proof was in the pudding, so to speak. Buyers paid high prices for my uniformity silver pelts at the auction houses. And I sold breeding stock all over the world.

In London, England, one full-length garment made from my silver fox skins retailed for $25,000 in 1986.

I expanded the number of foxes that I kept each year, while perfecting my one mutation of silver by selective breeding. That I had learned how to do with my racing pigeons for years.

I genetically enhanced the colour, texture, size and density. I eventually produced more uniformity in all my pelts. My bundles of fur sold for some of the highest prices at the auction houses around the world. My dream of having a successful farm had come true.

Cobb Silver Fox Ranch, 1980, five years after our arrival in New Brunswick. I now had a farm producing a living and food for my family. My dream come true.

Our second dream of having lots of children was not going as well. My wife was not able to carry our babies to full term. And it took a large toll on both of us. We did not know why.

After my wife and I were married she became pregnant but miscarried when we were living in Quebec. My wife told me it was because of my driving too fast on rough roads home after a weekend camping and scuba diving on the east coast. But that was not the cause at all. I was to find out differently from her gynecologist years later when she was pregnant with our daughter. She had an incompetent cervix from a previous procedure when we first met in Montreal.

In New Brunswick we had our first son Jeffrey on August 25, 1975, born premature.

Between 1976 and 1979, Dawn miscarried in her second trimester once more, and had two children so premature

194   IAN COBB

that they could not be saved. Vanessa was born on June 18, 1976 and Anthony on September 18, 1977.

At both burials, I was the only person in attendance; they were very tough days for me. Dawn was still in hospital. I personally carried each little styrofoam box from the hearse and laid it into the pre-dug hole. With tears I said the Lord's Prayer, put a fist full of dirt on top of the Styrofoam box and then spoke to the grave digger to make sure the grave would be filled in right away. I had never been to a funeral before in my life, but these two days were two very emotional days for me. For years I asked my wife to go to their graves with me but she never would. I went to their graves on their birthdays a few times. The last time that I went there with my best friend Andrée was in 2010. I had intentions of digging them up and burying them in the grave plot that I now own in Belleville. But I was told there would be nothing left to bring back.

In these later years, I have been thinking a lot about what Dawn must have been going through at this time and I can understand her not visiting these graves. Pregnant so often with such sad outcomes, these must have been very difficult for her.

Dawn and I had no idea why she could not carry full term so I started checking out about adopting a baby. Dawn told me she did not want to bring strangers' babies into the home. I did not understand this attitude but I was persistent. I pressured her and I finally convinced her to have a meeting with the New Brunswick government adoption agency with me. They interviewed us a few times in our home and we were approved to be adoptive parents in 1979.

On March 6th 1980, we adopted a baby boy and named him Graham. We were very thrilled, including his big brother Jeffery who was five by then.

The very night that we brought Graham home and put him in his crib, we went downstairs and I asked Dawn if she wanted to have a drink to celebrate. She said no, because she was now pregnant again. Well, that was good news. But this time, I was going to get involved when she next had her appointment with her gynecologist.

I told the doctor point blank about Dawn's past problems of not being able to carry her pregnancies to full term and I wanted to know why and what he was going to do differently for her this time around. So that we would not have to go through this disappointment and trauma again. He told us that she had an incompetent cervix and that was why she could not carry to full term properly. We put a plan in place that he would suture her up and in the final weeks she would also be put flat on her back in hospital until the baby was born.

That is just what we did and daughter Lisa was born January 1st 1981.

With many years of losing children that we both wanted and now I finally knew why. It was because of having that abortion done when we first met in Montreal. Things might be very different if the procedure was carried out today. I carry a lot of guilt and sadness to this very day that I was part of this decision and procedure that cost us all these babies. It took a lot out of our relationship. I did not have the same respect for myself and her after I realized what we had done. I just buried my guilt in working as hard as I could. I really didn't know how Dawn was coping.

There was not much time for us to do things together. We were both working hard to make a life. I did not know another way of ever getting ahead, except to keep working and devising ways to be more productive daily. While I was still young and strong, I needed to work hard while I still could.

My fear of being unsuccessful, old and poor, drove me daily. It was an obsession for me. I would unfairly push my wife into being more productive with me as well. Saying the good times would come later. We now had three children and I was going to make sure there was money for them to go to university and they not have to struggle like I did, without an education. Even so, I could not tell her about the extent of my lack of education, my illiteracy. Nor could I tell my children.

I learned new ways every day by trying different things, but I could only progress at my level of comprehension. Things that I could not do or understand I would have others, including my wife, do for me. Not only did my wife work part-time bringing in much needed cash for the family, she always helped me on the ranch when I needed a hand. But she was not always a happy camper being a farmer's wife. Especially when my frustration got the better of me having to get others to help me do things that I just could not. I was certainly not a multi-tasker, and I became quite frustrated at not being able at times. I had to have my wife help me do some things she really did not want to do and she should not have had to. This was not the life she imagined or wanted. But without her help, especially in the early years, I do not know how I would have made it.

I was learning by trial and error and had many sleepless nights with worry. I just could not afford to make mistakes that would cost me or put me out of business. There was no one else but me to share my thoughts with; no one else thought like I did in the first place. So I could not explain what I was doing. I just told people what to do. This was not the best way to keep a loving relationship going.

We now had three children, but I never forgot about my daughter Shannon that I made a promise to when she was only a week or so old. I told her that I would find her one day. I searched to find a private investigator that would help me locate her. I hired a former RCMP officer that had a private investigation business in Vancouver. I gave him

Homesteading, 1980.

all the information that I had about Shannon's mother, her aunt Pearl who I had understood was raising Shannon, but I did not know her last name. At one point he called me and thought he had found her in Vancouver, but wrong birthdate. He said he would keep looking and would get back to me if he had something positive to tell me.

With Jeffrey and Graham.

Dawn and myself with Jeffrey and Graham.

MY HEADWINDS TO FREEDOM

Christmas.

Jeffrey loved animals.

IAN COBB

Jeffrey and one of our cows.

My first load of chickens going to market in 1979 - $1300.00.

The boys on their bikes.

IAN COBB

CHAPTER
13
Home of the Silver Fox

I was still getting lots of grain from time to time by sweeping out the boxcars down at the hump yard. Enough to help feed the hens, chickens, sheep, pigs, and pigeons.

Paul, my neighbour from across the way, had a private abattoir at his friend's farm. He would go to the livestock auction sale Sussex N.B. or buy a few cattle locally to butcher and sell meat around the area. He took me with him a few times to the livestock sale and to his abattoir. I saw how he hung the cattle up, skinned, cleaned and butchered them. That gave me a great idea. I made a couple of signs, advertising my new province-wide, Dead Livestock service. I asked permission to put my signs on the walls at the auction sale.

Every day there was a cow in someone's barn dying. If a farmer went out in the morning and found a dead animal in his barn, he was not permitted to milk his cows until it was removed. In the winter the ground was too frozen to bury in and it took time and expense to dig a hole and bury them in the summer. They just had to call me and I would pick them up for $20. If I needed to put an animal down before taking it away I charged $5. I was the only one in the province to have a permit to carry my hunting rifle in my truck twelve months of the year.

This source of feed for the fox ranch took off that week. Phone calls came in to the house, I needed the address and to know that the farmer had a front end loader on his tractor. I brought them home, backed into my barn doorway. Hooked the animal up to a set of chain falls that was hanging from the barn ceiling beam and I just raised it up and drove out from under. I would skin it while hanging. Then I would roll the paunch out of the animal and into a barrel. I would then go to work cutting and chopping up the carcass. I would wheelbarrow the meat down to the pens and throw it in. The foxes would eat the bones clean. I picked up all the bones once a week and took them to the rendering plant for five cents a pound.

Not only that, I had a tractor trailer truck stop by every month to pick up all my cow and horse hides that I had salted down on the floor of my barn. He picked up hides from Halifax until he reached the tannery in Montreal. He paid cash, $50 each, a calf hide $20, cash. I would have five or six a month.

It was general agriculture knowledge among farmers around the world that you could not feed fish to animals because they would die. No one, including the veterinarians, could tell me exactly why this was so. They just said that it could not be done.

This was unbelievable for me to comprehend. I had seen foxes eating fish in the wild all over the place. There was no way I was buying into their nonsense.

So guess what I did? Yup! I went to speak to the fish packing plant managers. I found out that they were having to pay $60 a ton and take the waste themselves to be spread on fields that used it as crop fertilizer.

I made a deal with fish plants for the waste. They would phone me and I would pick up all their waste using my truck and they would pay me the $60 a ton. I bought four insulated plastic fish tubs. Each one could hold more than a 1000 pounds. Two tubs would fit on the back of my truck using their forklift. After I was loaded, they would put a few shovels of crushed ice on top before the cover was put on. I brought home many tons of herring, cod, flounder, and smelts. I fed it with no problem all year long. I also found out why I was the only one that could use it, but I never told anyone. I had this feed source all to myself, and I was producing top quality fur with it.

All other ranchers had expensive freezer rooms, grinders and mixers. They made the perfect percentage feed formula that was designed by the professionals that they fed in a paste form. I wondered to myself, who was making this formula in the wilderness for the scavengers?

Other ranchers ground chicken, eggs, other meats and cereals and mixed them the way the formula was designed by agricultural nutritionists. Well, me being more of a naturalist than a farmer and also not having the big money that I would need to build a feed kitchen and freezer room, I just chunk fed whatever I could find. Just like the wild animals did in the woods.

So no one was using the huge volume of fish waste but me. The packing plants all along the coast were producing tons of this feed that no one else could use but me.

I found and was given for no cost a huge pile of old galvanized maple syrup pails. They did not use them anymore. Today they just use connected solid lines to drain the sap from the trees to the holding tanks. I cut and folded these pails into hoppers to fit through the front of my fox pens. I fed a total ration pig pellet only once a week into the door hopper to supplement my foxes' diet of tons of free meat and fish. You can see my son Jeffrey feeding pellets to the foxes in the picture on the following page.

My oldest son Jeffrey holding his pet fox Vicky and feeding a pig pellet
to the foxes in their door hoppers.

IAN COBB

After pelting season, the breeders are kept in these wire pens
to absorb more sunlight as the length of daylight increases,
which brings them into heat or estrus.

IAN COBB

After breeding, females are put into the sheds with a kennel to whelp their pups in, at the end of gestation.

Dawn taking pelts in and out of two sided pelt cleaning drum.

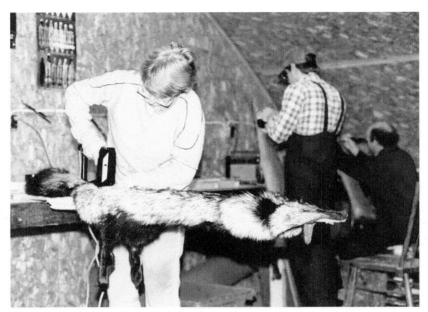

Dawn is stapling pelts to the drying boards, while the men scrape
and prepare more pelts for her to staple.

Some years later, I used another province agriculture
laboratory that I will not name and where I had a personal
friend working. I explained my theory to them, which
made perfect sense to me. But I needed proof from a lab
to confirm what I had discovered. I had discovered the
answer to why animals died when fish was introduced in
their diet. But I needed a lab to prove my theory correct. I
have never made this public before because I did not want
to share my feed source of fish, which was sure to happen
if I disclosed the true fact of why these animals died eating
fish. This is the first time this has ever been made public. It
was not fish that was killing animals at all. Although others
were feeding a very good feed formula, they were mixing
everything together. When fish was added to the mix, the
fish oils after sitting only thirty minutes in the feed would
neutralize all the thiamine, and some other vitamins in the
cereal base feeds. This essential nutrient was now void in

the animals' diet, and the animals would die. So they just eliminated fish from the feed altogether.

Well, in my operation, I was chunk feeding all my meat and fish. And I was feeding my cereal nutrients separately in the pellet hoppers that I made. I used a hog grower pellet, and only once a week. The fish oil chemical reaction did not take place in the animal's gut when it was fed separately. And so the animal was able to absorb all the nutrients it needed when fed in this manner.

It was a lot of physical work to be sure, but I was producing a pelt or breeding stock for a total overhead cost of only $13 each. My auction sale price per pelt was becoming greater as well, by my genetic breeding method. And I invented a method of breeding, using artificial insemination that had never been done before with wild animals. Farmers started arriving from Europe, mostly from Belgium and Holland, as well as USA and Canada and they purchased breeding stock from me for over $1000 each. I have never divulged my information about my fish discovery to anyone before I wrote it here today.

Each day of my life has always been an adventure. I never know in advance how my day will start or finish. Here is an example of one of my more normal days.

On different occasions over the years, I received phone calls to pick up dead livestock, "to feed to my ranch," that had died at the Dorchester Maximum Security Penitentiary. They had their own prison farm inside the guarded area where some of the inmates worked. I had to go to the back of the prison to pick up these dead cows. I passed through two guarded gates to enter the farm grounds. On my third visit over a couple years to this facility, to pick up another dead cow, the guards knew me and knew I was coming that morning to pick up. I went through with just a good morning at both gates to the guards who just opened the gates and I drove over to where the dead cow was lying on the ground. Four or five farm working prisoners came over with the farm tractor to load this animal on my truck. I always used a large chain to wrap around the animal and attach it to the front end bucket of the tractor. They would raise up the cow and I would just back the truck under. I always kept my chain that I used behind the seat of my half ton truck.

Once the men and tractor were beside me, and as I was standing outside my truck. I opened the door of my truck to pull the seat forward to get my chain out. It was then that a cold fear hit me that ran up and down my spine and I instantly pushed my seat back, hopped on the seat and started my truck, at the same time telling the prisoners that I forgot something at the gate. I'll be right back, I said. Getting back to the gate I jumped out and told the guards that I had really screwed up. I had mistakenly not remembered that I had my high power 30.06 hunting rifle behind my seat all the time. I was the only person in the province of New Brunswick to have a license to carry my rifle behind my seat in a case, twelve months of the year which I used for putting down farm animals at times, for my dead livestock pick up business.

One guard immediately phoned the front gate and office and told them; the other guard hopped into my truck and escorted me around to the front door of the prison. When we got to the front, two more guards came out and down the front stairs. They took my rifle out of my truck and carried it back up the stairs with me while the other guard searched my truck and stayed with it. After we entered all the locked doors inside of the prison, we entered a heavy barred room where my rifle was secured in a steel locker. I was escorted back to where I had left the prisoners and tractor and we then loaded the cow on the back of my truck. I was again escorted back to the front gate to pick up my rifle.

Inside the front main gate office I had to sign a paper that I pretended to read. And I was told in no uncertain terms that I was not permitted to pick up there ever again. And how could anyone be that stupid and still be walking the planet, I was told. I was red in the face with embarrassment all the way back home. And I never received another call from them again. I really did not blame them, when you think for a minute what could have happened. But I did think that it was a little bit of their responsibility to ask everyone going into such a place if they might have a weapon of any kind in the vehicle.

Years earlier when I was working on pipeline construction in western Canada, the pipeline right away crossed many farms and ranches. When I could, I talked to many farmers and ranchers about their different operations. There was some information that I picked up from a few of them that I implemented on my fox ranch in New Brunswick as well as on my mink ranch in Prince Edward Island when I constructed it there. Some of these farmers were very concerned about the noise from our large machinery working while we crossed their farms and ranches and especially if we had to do any blasting of rock for the ditch. I was told that aviation as well had a dramatic effect on different types of livestock and poultry operations. When planes or helicopters flew too close over their farms, hens stopped laying, chickens would bunch up into corners and suffocate themselves. High strung and nervous animals when pregnant would abort their pregnancies.

So when I built my operations, I had a letter written and delivered to the Federal Department of Transport and the Military explaining and giving the coordinates of my fox ranch. I was told that I had to paint chrome yellow and black stripes on top of the roofs of my sheds, which I did. I was also told that it was now illegal for any aviation to approach within a mile of my marked operation.

LOOKING the cameraman straight in the eye is one of the foxes on the farm of Ian Cobb of Salisbury. Mr. Cobb, holding the animal, has had problems with low-flying helicopters. [Photo By Bill Rumming]

IAN COBB

Now in New Brunswick there is an air force military training base a couple hundred miles north of my ranch location. I had this letter of mine sent to them so as to protect my investment. But I suffered the misfortune of having a helicopter fly directly over my ranch while I was feeding my foxes. I looked up to see two young pilots that were just in training flying down the river in a Huey helicopter. They saw my ranch and came over it to investigate. They were so close that I saw that the pilot was wearing blue tinted sunglasses. The reverberation from the helicopter made the water that was on the field at that time from snow melt, dance in ripples. I waved at them frantically, motioning them away as they looked at me.

It was spring and all my female foxes were in their nest boxes with their young pups. I saw my females come out of their nest boxes and start running around frantically. Some had pups in their mouths trying to protect them from this terrific noise. Hiding them in the corners of the wire pens in the snow that was still left on the ground. The whole ranch was in chaos with foxes running up the wire pens trying to get away from this horrific noise. Running with pups in their mouths trying to protect them. Many pups died that day. Their nest boxes were now like being inside a bass drum. And the females were trying to protect their young.

I wrote down the numbers of the helicopter and raced to my telephone calling the tower at the Moncton Airport to report the mishap. They told me that they were a civilian service but would contact the military to advise. After a few days the young pilot phoned me himself to apologize. I asked him how I would go about putting in a claim for my losses. He gave me the base commander's phone number, who I called immediately. All he said was his legal team would be in touch with me.

I never heard back until months later. Only after I had sent them a lawyer's letter, claiming $50,000 in losses. At the same time getting in touch with the media. After a long time of trying to do the correct thing to get some compensation from this arrogant legal department of the government, I took this matter into my own hands and beat the buggers. The Canadian military produced my letter that I had sent to them years earlier, to protect my investment from just such an occurrence. It had a received military stamp on it, dated one day after the helicopter fly over. I had sent it years earlier than the official stamped received date. If they wanted to play that game, then I could play a bigger game, and I did and won the day.

Now If you remember around 1978 when the USA was conducting cruise missile testing, in the Canadian north, the native people of that area were complaining about the large negative effect the overflights of these missiles were having on wildlife. Both the Canadian and American governments would only answer the allegations by saying that there was no such proof of any damage from the overflights of cruise missiles or any other type of flights. So I took it upon myself to get in touch with the Pentagon in the USA directly, and I told them that I now had the proof of overflight damages to wildlife and sent pictures of my dead fox pups to them. I also told them that I would be inviting the CBC from Canada and CNN from the USA news television networks to my ranch, if I did not receive a positive response to my claim for compensation for damages done from overflights of my fox ranch.

It was only four days later that a courier drove from Ottawa, directly to my ranch. He knocked on my door and I signed for receiving my check of $50,000. Funny how things work if you are in the right and use your imagination

Fox pups lost,

By CHUCK McCREADY
Staff Writer

SALISBURY (Special) — Whop. Whop. Whop. Whop. Helicopter blades slapping at the air alerted local residents that another military exercise was in progress.

WHOP. WHOP. WHOP. The wide blades, with their high angle of attack, set up a ground resonance, disturbing to humans, but causing complete frenzy among foxes on area ranches.

When the exercise was over, according to area fox ranchers, animals valued at more than $50,000 were dead, and they hold the department of national defence directly accountable for that loss.

Rancher Ian Cobb said the military at CFB Gagetown deny any responsibility in the incidents, said to have occurred March 29 and April 1, but he has documentation and witnesses to prove his case and will take the issue to court if necessary.

Cobb's loss of about 24 fox is valued at up to $25,000, a figure verified by the Moncton area agriculture department representative as a reasonable figure. Fox ranchers Lawrence Price and Bruce Williams, also both of Salisbury, suffered similar losses.

Ironically, Williams was himself a military pilot and helicopter, flight instructor for eight years prior to turning to fox ranching, and he's fully aware of the effect of ground resonance on livestock and of the precautions taken to avoid such stress.

Williams was away on business when the over-flights are said to have occurred, but upon returning he found evidence that a major disruption had taken place.

"I had 17 females due to whelp that week, and from those 17 I raised seven pups, when normally it would have averaged 34. I found slaughtered pups the day after the incident, dead and mutilated, and in my own mind I couldn't justify it," Williams said.

Fox are naturally high strung, he added, and a female seeks full security in hiding her litter. Ranchers don't even take tractors near the kennels when the animals are whelping because frightened females will often kill their young.

"You can imagine the chaos created when a chopper goes over with a terrific noise seeming to come from nowhere," Williams said.

CFB Gagetown base information officer Ross Ingram said Tuesday one helicopter was flying in the area on April 1.

"It was flying at 1,300 feet, which is 800 feet higher than the ministry of transport requires," Ingram said. "The aircraft was flying by instrument flight rules, so the direction and angle of the craft was dictated by radio communication.

"Whenever possible we avoid fox and mink farms. In the CFB Chatham ready room they're all marked on the map and we make an effort to avoid them.

"As for responsibility in the incident, our legal people will be investigating and making a statement, so it would be improper to comment at this time."

Cobb, meanwhile, says 25 to 30 village residents can verify the claim of 1,300

FOX RANCHER IAN COBB

I look at this picture below, with all these papers in front of me and I just can't help cracking up! At that time, I could hardly read, but I looked good.

in getting others to do the right thing. Some people say "you can't fight city hall. If you are in the right, I say, yes you can, and you should."

Now that we were coming ahead financially, I was able to enjoy a little more time with my pigeons. Most times when I drove a fair distance to pick up fish waste or dead livestock, I would bring a few baskets of my pigeons to release, maybe thirty or forty of them at a time. Although there was not a club close enough to race with, I always went into young bird races in different locations. How these young bird races worked was a flyer would breed from his best pairs and band their young birds at about ten days old with a special race band that had to be purchased from a certain club holding the race. Before these young gained their flight, they would ship them to a specific race loft, anywhere in the world. All the pigeons were kept in one loft and once they gained their flight they would orient themselves to that specific location by circling in a flock and imprinting on their brain the exact location of their home on the planet. Their own G.P.S. system. That racing club or committee would train all the birds each day until race day. Only one race was held for those birds in the fall. All the pigeon owners would show up race day to enjoy the day together, bet on their birds and to watch the birds arrive at the loft.

Most young bird races are around 400 miles in distance or so. And there could be a 100 or up to 2000 birds in the large events around the world. I sent some young birds to a few different races over the years.

On one occasion in 1980, the club in Fredericton, New Brunswick was holding a young bird classic race in September, from Montreal Quebec to Fredericton. I bred four birds for that race, and they were trained along with the rest. On the day of the race the weather at release point was clear and sunny. But as the race progressed the birds encountered a severe hurricane storm in the northern United States. Depending on weather, head wind or tail wind, pigeons can fly 35 to 60 miles an hour. On this race day there were no day birds that had arrived. And the race was only 340 miles in a straight line. There were only seventy-five birds in this race that day. The first bird arrived at 11:30 am the next day. The second bird arrived at 11:35 am and the third bird arrived at 12:48 am. All three of these winners were mine that day. I won $2188.10 in prize money. Only one other bird ever showed up a week or two later.

That was the toughest race that I have ever been in. But I have to tell you, I sold a lot of my birds for breeding stock all over Canada and the United States once this race was published in The Pigeon Racing Federation Yearbook. I would ship breeding stock to pigeon flyers by Canada Post Air Mail, the same way that poultry chicks are sent to different farms from the hatcheries.

Also talking about my pigeons, in 1984 it was the province of New Brunswick's bicentennial year. We were having a visitor attend our Canada Day Celebrations, from Rideau Hall in Ottawa, The Right Honorable Governor General of Canada, Madame Jeanne Sauve. I contacted her office and asked if my racing homing pigeons might be used to deliver her bicentennial message to the New Brunswick Lieutenant Governor as she had planned to do. With microfilm of her message attached to my small flock of pigeons, they flew her Bicentennial message from Ottawa to my loft in New Brunswick. The media were all there when my birds arrived, and her message was read to the province.

I am holding our 1st place winning pigeon and my son Jeffrey is holding our 1st place trophy. My family got the prize money check for first, second and third place of $2188.10.

IAN COBB

New Brunswick
Bicentennial
Commission

Commission du
Bicentenaire du
Nouveau-Brunswick

Post Office Box 1984
Fredericton, N.B. E3B 5H1
Telephone: (506) 472-1984

C.P. 1984
Fredericton, N.-B. E3B 5H1
Téléphone: (506) 472-1984

July 18, 1984

Mr. Ian Cobb
Salisbury, N.B.
E0A 3E0

Dear Mr. Cobb:

On behalf of the New Brunswick Bicentennial Commission
I want to thank you for participating in the 1984 Bicentennial
Pigeon Race from Ottawa to New Brunswick. The spirit of the
competition, and the dedication your winged messengers showed,
truly complements our province's Bicentennial and highlighted
the 1984 Canada Day celebrations.

The delivery of the bicentennial message from Governor
General Madame Jeanne Sauvé to New Brunswick Lieutenant-
Governor George F. Stanley could not have been entrusted to any
more faithful messengers. As the message on the microfilm is
very difficult to read without appropriate equipment, I am
pleased to enclosed a copy of the message of the Governor
General.

I hope that you enjoyed participating in this very special
race and that you will have the opportunity to participate again
in many other Bicentennial celebrations this year.

Sincerely,

Alfred Landry, Q.C.
Chairman

Enc.

A thank you from the New Brunswick Bicentennial Commission.
Our pigeons were true ambassadors.

MY HEADWINDS TO FREEDOM   221

My ranch and home were on the Petitcodiac River about twenty miles upstream from The Bay of Fundy. The Fundy tide, when coming in, would come over twenty miles upriver and past my place in a wave. It is called the tidal bore. The mudflats all along the tidal bore produced a small mud shrimp. I loved watching the billions of migrating shorebirds flocking and feeding on these mud shrimp when they would stop on their migration for a week or two in both spring and fall. At the mouth of the Petitcodiac River are the world renowned Flower Pot rocks that have been carved out of the rock wall shoreline over many thousands of years.

Beside growing most of my family's food of, pork, lamb, beef, chicken and eggs, I would get a fair amount of seafood from the surrounding ocean waters. In the Bay of Fundy that was not far away, we could jig for cod and fish for other species. These rich cold waters produce the finest lobster in the world. Most Canadians do not know the difference in this great tasting lobster, because most of it gets shipped and served in the finest hotels and restaurants in London, Paris, New York and other cities around the world. The other sand bottom feeding lobsters have a totally different diet.

One of my favorites are scallops which, as a diver, I could pick off the bottom and bring up to the surface in a diver's catch bag. Now, the Bay of Fundy has the highest tides in the world, some sixty feet high twice a day. So as a diver it was a large challenge to dive safely, other than at slack tide. This would give a diver only about an hour and a half of bottom time. If we dove from a boat and were late surfacing with the tide now running, we could find ourselves half a mile away from our boat. And another thing to be aware of was that in the Bay, a fog could roll in very quickly at any time. If that happened we would not be able to find our way to the boat. So we always carried whistles attached to our life vests.

Fishing in the abundant waters of the Bay of Fundy.

Millions of years ago lava flowed from the shoreline and across the floor of the sea, leaving these two hundred foot high solid walls of rock and also forming long fingers of lava rock out into the bay across the sea floor. Scallop fishermen drag large drag nets on the floor to harvest these scallop shells. But they cannot drag their gear across these fingers of lava without ruining their gear. So they stayed a long way clear of these areas, leaving these virgin bottom beds of scallops between the massive long fingers of rock. I discovered these virgin beds of scallops that had never been harvested before. Some of the shells were twelve and fourteen inches across. These scallops had to be cut in half to get them into the frying pan and to cook them properly. We cleaned and froze many pounds to have with garlic butter over the winters.

I never seemed to find the time to spend on or in the water as much as I would have liked to. The ranch and my children always came first. Raising three kids, who we kept busy in all the local sports and community activities, I was not able to take the family on vacations or trips with so many animals to feed and water each day. As we grew the operation, my wife and kids would help me out with chores most days, especially Jeffrey. At even a very young age he was very responsible. Jeff was five years older than the other two, and when I was away getting fish or something else, I knew that all the ranch would be watered and any leaking pails would be changed.

I promised my children that when they wanted to go to university or any other post-secondary education they just had to show me a diploma and I would write a check for the total school years cost and expenses. The farm gave us everything, but there sure was a lot of labour involved and I just hoped for family fun days later on.

With so much labour collecting, cutting, chopping, and feeding fish and dead livestock, I was ripe for the picking when a salesman from the largest feed company in Canada knocked on my door. He told me that they had developed a total ration fox pellet specifically developed on their experimental fox ranch in Ontario over a two-year period with fantastic results. They would like to supply my ranch for a full year with their new pellet at no cost to me so they could use my operation as advertising in how well their new fox feed worked. I thought that by cutting my labour in half, and the fact that I was already set up with pellet feeders on my pens, it should free me up a little more to do other things and expand my operation. After all, they had already tested this feed on their foxes for two years with great results. This sure sounded like a very nice offer. Well I should have known, If it sounds too good, it probably is.

So in the late fall I had put all my breeders in their outdoor runs and started to feed them this total ration pellet. Well, it sure gave me more time to do my fleshing and drying of my pelts. After skinning when the fur is prime in the fall, all the pelts were put into bags and stored in freezers until all pelting was finished. Then we took them out and started scraping them and putting them on boards for drying.

After a couple of months of my breeding stock being on this new feed, the first thing that I noticed, without a lot of concern, was that they were a little late to come into season or estrus. Most of them we were able to breed that year, but we had a few that never even came into heat at all. So that was my first red light of concern. At their due date to have their pups, some of the females had skipped, not producing any litter at all. That was second concern. I phoned the feed company to report this and to ask if they had this problem as well. They said they did not have any problems at all. Well, after it was time to wean my pups, we put them all in the furring sheds and continued on with this feeding program. I have a keen eye for signs of the health of any animal on a daily basis. I always examined the stools that had fallen through the wire floor, the clarity of the eye and the overall appearance. My larger growing pups would mostly be the males and were not as clear of eye as they should be and were not filling out like they should have. They were thinner and more lethargic than they should be.

I called the feed company again and was told that some other smaller fox ranches were on this feed program as well. And they were not having any problems. Within a week I had two dead pups in the pens and many more looked not well. I called the feed company again and this time I demanded for their nutritionist and management to come to my ranch immediately. The answer back was that I was the only ranch to be having this problem. I then told them that a few other farmers in my area had bought breeding stock from me and were following my lead in this feed program as well. And two of them had mortality as well.

It was time to act and fast. I raced to the coast and picked up tons of fish waste and picked up dead livestock as well. I did my own autopsies on the pups that had died to find that they had very little fat and their hearts were anemic, pale in colour. They looked like they were starving. But they had eaten a lot of pellets. I lost a few more pups over the next week but I got the problem stopped soon after introducing the red meat and fish again.

Finally a representative from the head office feed company showed up at my ranch after I had a lawyer send a letter of intent to sue. I gave him an ear full as I learned that the company never had tested this feed on foxes at all. I told him that my losses were very substantial and I would be sending them a very large invoice. I told him that I was selling breeding stock for $1000 each and that this year I could not, because I would not know how defective my pups might be if sold that year for breeders. I took the average number of pups produced each year by me and I wanted $1000 each for the difference produced this year. They had ten days in which to get back to me before I called the media and filed a lawsuit. They told me they were not liable.

Now, the war was on.

I produced three witnesses who told the judge at the hearing that they were on my front porch when the company representative told me his company tested the feed on their research farm in Ontario for two years with great results. I produced three farmers that were on the same feed program as myself and suffered the same problems. It took me nearly two years until they agreed to settle out of court. I was willing in the early days to settle for half of what I received in the end. When you are right you fight! This helped me build my fox and mink ranch in P.E.I.

I also discovered why these perfect formula pellets were not working, and that I will try to explain here now.

I always did my own autopsies on any of my animals that happened to die. I gained a lot of knowledge from doing so. Foxes produce very strong digestive juices naturally. These juices break down all kinds of very tainted meat in order for them to use the nutrient. These juices are released into the gut with the first smell or taste of raw meat by the fox, the same way your own stomach might growl when hungry as you walk into a kitchen with great smelling food cooking. So when I was feeding raw fish or meat to my foxes, they could break it all down in their gut to use. The digestive juices would release. Just like what happens in the water with a shark frenzy when they first have the scent of raw blood in the water that releases a hormone from the brain to feed.

Well, when the meat meal in a pellet has already been cooked along with the rest of the feed formula, the natural digestive juices in the fox do not get released into the gut to break down the meat meal in the pellet to use, and it just passes through the animal not broken down. This nutrient passes unused and the fox is denied this nutrient, causing malnutrition and a slow starvation death. Full grown foxes can just get enough nutrient to get by on. But a growing pup needs to receive a terrific amount of food to be fully grown and mature by fall.

Another feeding problem that I had to overcome was at one point my largest fox pups started to take seizures in their pens, and I had no clue to why this was happening. Only after one had died and I autopsied it did I notice a brownish and slightly pasty substance around the kidneys and heart. I sent it away to the agriculture college to be analyzed. Two more died that week. It came back from the lab as calcium. I spoke to the veterinarians about this, and they told me my foxes died of over calcification of the heart. I said okay, then why were they taking seizures first? That is a brain disorder. They did not know and told me there was no money to research this matter for me.

But I thought I knew the problem. I was feeding tons of fish waste and bone racks, so that must be the problem. So I cut back on feeding as much fish. It did not happen again for a month and I thought I had the correct defence cutting back on the fish. But my pups started to take seizures again. This time I spoke to a different agriculture college telling them about the seizures. And they asked me to ship the brain matter in formaldehyde solution to them, which I did. It came back saturated with calcium. So I cut back further on the amount of fish racks that I was feeding.

It was not until I was picking up a dead cow one day that I saw a veterinarian at this farm giving a very large syringe injection of a white substance to another cow in its belly vein. I asked the vet what he was giving to this cow and why. He told me that these Holstein cattle are bred for very massive milk producing size udders. And sometimes their body calcium is drained and they die from milk fever and mastitis. In order to try and save them, they often inject huge vials of pure calcium into their belly vein. But some of them die even after the treatment. And I would pick up these dead cows for feed. Growing pups would take on all this calcium.

So now I knew how my fox pups were saturated with calcium and taking seizures. My faster growing pups would take on all this calcium because their bodies were growing, while my adult foxes would just pass the excess.

My pups, while taking seizures, would thrash around in their pens, hitting their heads against the posts and concuss themselves. Once concussed, some of them took a very long time to come around and would only drink water and sleep for some days before they started to come back to their normal activity. Just by looking in their eyes and watching their actions I could sometimes tell that they were still concussed days later.

This is what started me thinking about sports concussions and our military personal with post traumatic brain injuries.

It was only when I retired, moved to Ontario and was racing my pigeons did I start telling people about my concussion findings years earlier. A medical university was looking for a navigational specie and bought a lot of my pigeons for research on brain disorders. I expressed and explained my findings on my ranch many years earlier to pathologists. This led to getting funding, mostly in the States, and proving my theory on post-concussion. It took off from there and is still being worked on around the globe and refined today.

Here is an article I wrote after gaining my literacy.

Published by Ian Grant Cobb—2009
After concussion, severe pain, depression, and it can kill.

What is a concussion? as comprehended and explained by myself.

I have been involved as a lay person with research pertaining to neurology at a major medical university. Before that I had picked up a lot of information over the years, working first with veterinary pathologists when I was doing my own autopsies and research on my fox and mink ranch in New Brunswick, because of a calcium problem that occurred while feeding dead livestock and fish waste on my fox ranch.

Since retirement and moving to Ontario, I have been involved with neurology research with a major medical university. Only as the handler of my homing pigeons involved in the research of Alzheimer, Parkinson's and Dementia, at this medical university.

After some time, I offered some of my former findings from my own animal autopsies on my ranch, about my foxes taking seizures from over calcification, and concussing themselves.

I do not profess to be an expert on the subject pertaining to concussion, but I will try to explain, the best that I can, what happens to the brain cells that have been concussed inside the skull. And why one must stay completely resting after a concussion.

The very soft brain cells, when violently thrown against the skull, are damaged and each neuron releases a potassium chemical out of the brain cell. Leaving a void. Calcium that is always present around the outside of the cells, seeps into the cells, replacing the potassium as a defensive mechanism.

This calcium is what gives the chemical imbalance to the brain and is what causes a sedation, effect, pain and damage that can lead to despair and suicide in some. Until all of this calcium leaves the brain cells completely, and it can take a long time, depending on how much calcium has been taken into each cell. The patient is left extremely vulnerable to permanent brain damage, as the calcium will instantly solidify upon second impact, killing those cells.

Even a hard coughing spell, light, and exercise can cause severe pain and damage. Complete rest is needed.

These damaged cells have to be cleared completely of this calcium before one can resume normal activity to avoid the calcium from solidifying, causing more serious consequences, including permanent brain damage and even death.

This is very acute in young people under the age of 24 as the brain is still growing and developing.

Please, coaches, parents and military personnel, know this, every severe explosion or contact to the head can cause some cells to expel potassium and take on calcium. A second, even slight bump, with the cells still containing calcium, can be very serious even deadly.

— *Ian Cobb*

I think my journey from my close observations while fox farming to this article is a good illustration of how I have learned all my life. Especially when one can't read and has little formal education, observation and experimentation becomes the way one learns.

And I learned a lot from fur farming. Fur farming is very different, for sure. But really it is the same concept for all harvesting; when your crop is ready, it has to be picked when ripe. Foxes fur up for winter. Fur is prime for harvesting in late fall. We first picked out all the males and females that would be kept for breeding. All of the rest were put down humanely, by myself only, and pelted. We skinned them and put the pelts into feed bags and then put them into the freezer. Once that process was complete, it

Processing the pelts was hard work and often a family affair (above).
My second son Graham learning how to flesh pelts (below left).
My invention of drying pelts with the fur out (below right).

IAN COBB

was time to start taking some out of the freezer each day to start the fleshing and scraping to remove all of the fat from the skins. This is a very difficult job, the pelt can be torn very easily if you do not pay strict attention with your knife and scraper. Hands and arms take a real beating. Most nights my hands were so swollen from the work, that even with my fingers spread far apart, they were still touching each other. I used a lot of pain killers. I was able to buy and convert a mink fleshing machine into a fox fleshing machine. It was messy alright, but saved a lot of work. Before my barn was built, we had to skin and flesh the pelts in our basement as depicted here by my second son Graham who loved to help. I could not do homework with them, but I showed my kids work ethics.

You can see the notched boards with a paper sleeve over it, so the pelt would not stick to the board while drying.

After that we put the pelts into a two-sided drum that I made; it turned by using an electric motor. In the first side of the drum, I put hardwood sawdust, a cup of turpentine and a cup of hot water. As the pelts tumbled in this mixture, all the grease was removed from the pelt. They came out just like shampooing your hair; they came out very clean. After twenty minutes or so, we put them in the other wire side of the drum, to shake out all the sawdust onto the barn floor. We did about 20 pelts on each side at the same time.

Once we took them out of the shaker side, they were ready to pin and staple to the drying boards, fur facing out. Fur has always been dried on boards with the leather out and fur inside. But I discovered that not only was it labour intensive and very hard to turn pelts to fur out, once they were dry. It also caused some damage.

So I developed a way that I could dry about fifty skins in a 24-four hour period with the fur out. What I did was to use old steel bed frames for the frame of my drying racks. I built a plywood box on the top of the frame. I drilled holes in the bottom of the plywood box and inserted small air tubes. I screwed a hook beside each tube to hang the nose of the drying board onto. I used an old furnace fan to blow the air into the box and down each tube. All the boards I had previously notched out with my skill saw so the air from the nose air tube would blow inside of the pelts and down the notched boards, drying the skins. Inventing fur out drying saved a lot of time and damage.

This system worked like a charm. When we took out all the pins and staples and removed the skins from the boards, I would inspect them and comb them before putting them into cardboard shipping boxes to send to the different auction houses around the world. Once all the pelts had been shipped to auction, it was the start of the next breeding season. As I've described earlier in this book, this was a time of intense observation to ensure the best breeding results. This breeding season was the most important season of the year for our production. It took total concentration.

I was very busy but I also took an interest in community affairs. If you remember back a few years in this book, I wrote about me experiencing bigotry in the province of Quebec when I was trying to get work and experiencing it on the job. Well bigotry survives in every corner of the planet if you let it. I remember how inferior I felt by it. So when I see it anywhere or anytime, I stand up to it and these small-minded people.

In 1987 at the rural post office of the little village of Salisbury, a new bilingual Francophone postmaster was hired. I learned all about English bigots, the Orangemen they were called, who came to my village of Salisbury and, along with the locals, tried to get this very well-educated and efficient lady removed from her new position of postmaster because they wanted an English person in that position. There were about a hundred people along with the local member of The New Brunswick Legislature, carrying signs and chanting for her removal just because she was French and, mind you, she spoke perfect English. I thought this very unfair and I marched with my own homemade sign in her favour. I was the only one on my side of the street. Media was all there as well. The RCMP had to keep a few loudmouths away from taking my sign. They also had to

Canada   Postes
Post   Canada

CONFIDENTIAL

Salisbury, N.B.
EOA 3EO
September 9th, 1987

M. Ian Cobb
R.R.# 2
Salisbury, N.B.
EOA 3EO

Dear Sir:

My expression of gratitude for your stand during my recent ordeal is way beyond expression.

You are one Canadian who must have been noticed across Canada. You and I share this "strong" belief that no one should be discriminated against due to colour, shape or language.

I only hope that it did not cause you any harm; because I know some have received threats -- I thought of you and your family then and prayed you were in no danger.

Again, my sincere thanks for your constant support--may you and your family have a nice day!

Respectfully yours,

J. Lynn Levesque
POSTMASTER

Letter from J. Lynn Levesque to Ian Cobb after I took a stance against bigotry.

sit in their car near my ranch for a week or so guarding my barn and home, because some of the crowd came to my ranch with a can of gasoline and wanted to burn my farm and house. I did have my rifle loaded, but I did not have to bring it out. I received this very nice letter from her. She stayed with her job although she was scared. Last time I heard, she was an executive with Canada Post.

I also found this bigotry creeping into our New Brunswick schools. I tried to make a difference.

My friend Christopher, who now lives in B.C., said it best to me and he is absolutely correct with this comment. "The arrogance of the English Protestant and Catholic School Boards of Montreal and area, did not commence French Language instruction until Grade 3, and that was not daily, when we were in elementary in Montreal during the fifties. This in an 80%+ French speaking province. This arrogance resulted in 2 or 3 lost generations whom later found it difficult to impossible to be fluent in French, forcing many whom still loved the biculturalism of Quebec to leave for other parts of Canada and around the world."

Yes, I struggled with my illiteracy then for sure, but it would have been very helpful for me and many others to be able to speak French fluently in our own native province.

One afternoon I received a call from the private investigator in Vancouver that I had hired when Shannon would have been about sixteen years old. She was about nineteen now. He said to me, Ian, are you sitting down?

I found Shannon, he said.

Are you sure, I asked?

Yes he said. She is in Toronto, and she has been looking for you, he told me. I found her through her brother Albert who I located in Edmonton, Alberta. He drives taxi there.

The investigator gave me Shannon's phone number in Toronto. I was excited and very nervous. I wondered how

236   IAN COBB

Angered parent wants immersion move halted

By Charles Perry
Staff Reporter

Angered over plans by District 16 school board to replace total immersion with a combined immersion/core program, a concerned parent is trying to organize the other parents in a bid to halt the move, which is scheduled to go into effect in September.

Ian Cobb of Salisbury, who has a son in the total immersion program in Grade 5, said the district is signing away the opportunity for the area's children to be competitive in the job market. "English-speaking Canadians in New Brunswick can't even get a job in their own backyard today without fluency in both languages."

He said his oldest son is already fluently bilingual, but his three pre-school children will not get the same chance if the district goes ahead with plans to revise its total immersion program.

Under the district's proposal, which would replace the current immersion program, second language familiarization would be the aim in Grades 1 - 3, with 80 per cent English instruction and 20 per cent French. Intensive second language training will occur in Grades 4 through 6 with 80 per cent French and 20 per cent English instruction.

Second language training will progress in Grades 7 - 9 with French and English instruction being carried out on a 50/50 basis, while the last years of school will see the second language maintained through 80 per cent English and 20 per cent French instruction.

The program will not affect youngsters now in school, since all courses being taught will continue through to the graduation of the students involved. The district has offered early French immersion in Salisbury for 12 years and in Petitcodiac for six years.

"By the time a child is in Grade 4," said Cobb, "it is too late to expect him to become fluent in a second language. The district will try to soft-pedal the new program as being effective, but it isn't. You might as well give them a glass of water. It would have as much an effect."

Cobb said he was always disappointed that he was not given the chance to learn French when he was growing up in St. Lambert, Que. So, when he moved to New Brunswick to set up his fox farm business, he sought out a district where his children could take a total immersion program.

If he and other interested parents are unsuccessful in convincing the district to change its mind, he said he will move elsewhere. "My parents may not have had the foresight to fight for me to learn French. But my children will never be able to say I didn't fight for their future."

During a public meeting Wednesday night, said Cobb, the parents were given a sheet to sign which states: "Based on the information you have now, would you enrol your child in Option 1 (the name for the new combined program)?" The only other option, however, he said, is the regular English program.

The district was being "deceitful" in wording the statement in such a manner, by excluding the current total immersion program as an option, he said. And a great many people signed the sheet, not realizing that it would mean an end to the early immersion program in the district, he added.

In other words, said Cobb, the students have the option of either taking a seriously weakened French immersion program or an inadequate core course. If someone were to say "bonjour, monsieur" to a student in the core program, he explained, the student would only know the person was speaking French, and not Italian, but he would not know what he was saying.

At the same time, he conceded that there is a strong contingency in Albert County which opposes French instruction of any kind in the schools.

"I heard things during the public meeting which made the hair on my neck bristle. I didn't realize there were so many bigots in this area. A good many of them were concerned about English-speaking teaching positions being lost. I don't want (unilingual) English-speaking people teaching my children French. Total immersion is the only answer."

Such statements as "we don't want French driven down our throats" or "one week of French a week should be enough to satisfy those (French-speaking) bastards" emerged during the meeting, said Cobb. "No wonder Atlantic Canada is trailing the rest of the country," he said.

However, he said, once the people began to congregate into groups immediately after the session, he realized he was not alone in wanting the early immersion program retained in the district.

Cobb said about 10 or 15 of the parents there told him later that they supported him, but were "shy" about the idea of standing up and stating thier mind at the meeting.

"I'm sure there are a great many other parents in the district who feel the same way I do about the early immersion program. Many of them no doubt are planning to enrol children in the early immersion program and are not even aware this option is being taken away from them."

He urged anyone, who is interested in joining with him to keep the current French immersion program in place in the district, is urged to contact him. Now is the time to mount an attack to save the program, he said, adding "if we wait any longer, it is going to be too late."

From the Times-Transcript, January, 1986

was it she was looking for me and who had told her about me. What was she doing in Toronto? How was I going to start this conversation and what would I say? I waited for Dawn to get home from work and we had a long talk about all possible scenarios. I called Shannon the next afternoon. I was very surprised to hear a man's deep voice. I asked for Shannon and this fellow said she was not back from

MY HEADWINDS TO FREEDOM   237

work yet. He asked me who was calling, and I said Ian. Shannon's father, he asked? I nearly fell off my chair. He told me to call back around 6 pm when she would be home.

I called back and she answered the phone. I was mystified and had a lot of questions for her. She told me that she knew of me and she had a picture of me holding her as an infant. She had travelled from Calgary to Montreal searching for me. She spent some time there looking for me but, of course, I was in New Brunswick by then, while my whole family had moved to Ontario many years ago. And there was no one around who had heard of me. She then went to Toronto and shared an apartment with a fella from Newfoundland. We talked a while and I asked if I could fly to Toronto to meet her. We agreed to meet at a hotel where I booked a room.

Three or four days later, I was on a flight to Toronto. I was so excited one minute and nervous the next all the way. The poor gentleman sitting beside me on the plane got an ear full for the whole trip. I just did not shut up the whole time. It turned out that he was the Chief of Police of the city of Moncton, and his wife sat on the other side of him reading. When we landed, he told me that I had a very interesting life and he was very glad for me that I had found Shannon. He told me that if ever Shannon came to visit me in New Brunswick, he would love for me to bring her to meet him, at his office.

The minute I saw Shannon at the Toronto airport, I recognized her right away. She was a knock-out and the spitting image of my sister at that age. We went to my hotel and talked most of the night until we fell asleep. It was very emotional for me. I asked her to visit my family and my ranch in New Brunswick. My wife and children had always known that she was out there someplace and we were looking for her. Shannon did come for a visit that summer; it was great to have my four children together for the first time. And yes, I took Shannon into Moncton to visit the

I found my eldest daughter Shannon at 19 years old, after only holding her for one day after birth in Alberta in 1968. I promised her then that someday I would find her and I did after hiring a private investigator who looked for her for three years. Later she came to our ranch in N.B. and this is the first picture of her with her kid sister, Lisa. She also lived with us in Belleville Ont. and worked at our pet food store there before going back to Alberta to start her own family.

Chief of Police who gave Shannon a tour and two Moncton Police badges which I still have today.

My mother and father had been living in Burlington, Ontario for some years and my brother called me to let me know that my dad was failing and was now in hospital. I made plans to drive there with my children to see him and my mother. Shannon had expressed a desire to meet her grandparents someday. So when we drove to Ontario, we picked up Shannon who was now living in Toronto, and we all drove and stayed in a hotel in Burlington. When I saw my dad in hospital, I was shocked to see that this 6 foot, 220 lb. man, was now a bedridden skeleton of about 140 lbs. He was waiting to have a heart valve operation. After a couple of days visit, I dropped Shannon off at home in Toronto and we drove back to New Brunswick. It was only a few days later that I got the call in New Brunswick that my dad did not make it through the operation.

So many life changes in such a short time. And more were to come.

In 1987, four fur ranchers from Europe visited my ranch to see my operation, purchase breeding stock, and to find out how I was producing top fur for the global market differently. One of them wanted to emigrate from Holland to Canada and build a ranch, if he could find a suitable location. He specialized in mink but had foxes as well. He was impressed with the way I was operating and we started to formulate a plan. He found a farm for sale on Prince Edward Island and I helped him move his assets to that farm from Holland. We formed a partnership.

THIS AGREEMENT made this _21_ day of _____, A.D. 1988.

BETWEEN: PETER   of Howe   Bay,   Souris,
             Province   of   Prince   Edward   Island,
             (hereinafter called   ),
                    OF THE FIRST PART

AND: IAN COBB, of the Town of Salisbury,
             County of Westmorland and Province of
             New   Brunswick,   (hereinafter   called
             "Cobb"),
                    OF THE SECOND PART

WHEREAS QUINTESSENTIAL FOX CORP. LTD. (hereinafter referred to as "the company") is a body corporate, incorporated under the provisions of the Business Corporations Act of the Province of New Brunswick by Articles of Incorporation dated the 17th day of August, A.D. 1987.

AND WHEREAS the authorized capital of the company consists of 5000 common shares with a par value of $1.00 per share of which 100 are issued and outstanding as fully paid and nonassessible common shares of the company;

AND WHEREAS each of Peters and Cobb are at the date of this agreement the beneficial owner of shares in the company as follows:

        Peter   33 shares
        Ian Cobb   67 shares

Forming a new venture with a friend.

I could skin a lot of mink in a day. It would take me about three minutes to skin one. Of course we used a smaller board to pin the mink pelt to for drying. I stayed with producing only two colours of mink, demi-buff (which is a brown) and black. About this time I had a brain wave for another source of feed for my ranches, which worked out great. This was after seeing on the news one night all the commotion about the seal hunters skinning their seals on the ice. They were taking the pelt and leaving the carcass behind on the ice pack for polar bears and other scavengers. The Ministry of Fisheries then told the sealers that they had to bring the carcasses on their boats to shore as well. The problem was, where could they dispose of them?

I approached the Ministry and told them that if they put them into five-foot square insulated fish tanks and put some crushed ice on top before putting the lid on, I would pick them up and bring them to my ranches. My animals loved them and they were easy to cut up and feed.

Again, I took another waste product and turned it into a quality commercial product at very little cost while bringing foreign dollars into our Canadian economy. It gave me great pride to contribute to my country in this manner as well as acquiring free feed.

Beside our farm animals on our ranch in Salisbury, we kept a few pets as well. Once I took in a very friendly Egyptian goat that had a foot problem that the owner did not know how to treat, and he wanted to get rid of him. I got the problem cleared up within a few weeks. My son Graham took a shine to him and he called him Billy. He was a large type Egyptian goat that would follow us around the ranch, and Graham would ride on him as well. We later donated him to the famous petting zoo at Magnetic Hill in New Brunswick. Another pet was a young blue heron that had a wing problem and could not fly. We sure had lots of fish to feed to him. He would stay inside our high guard fence. By the end of that summer he was flying in and out of the ranch until it was time to migrate with his kind. We always had a few barn cats that kept the rodents away from the ranch and barn.

I also used the cats to raise some of my fox pups with. If one of my foxes had a litter of six or seven, sometimes the mother could not produce enough milk for all of them and I would take one or two pups out of the kennel and put them into one with one of the cats that had kittens. All I would do was rub the fox pups against some of the kittens to take on the kittens' scent. The mother cat would raise the fox pup as her own. They are great mothers. We did keep one fox pup as a pet that was raised by our house cat. My kids called her Vicky and she was a great pet for the kids to play with. The only problem with a fox pet is that their urine smells like skunk and they are difficult to train to use a litter box. But she loved affection and played with the kids. She would lie on her back just like a puppy would and loved to have her belly rubbed. But we had to keep her on the ranch outdoors most of the time.

And of course I always had my homing pigeons that my kids enjoyed as well.

All three of my children were good skaters, having the pond and all. The pond served as a hockey and skating rink for a lot of kids in the area. The boys played hockey and Lisa played ringette in Riverview. I coached hockey and I was a coordinator for minor hockey in Riverview where they had a great program. The kids all played softball in Salisbury in the summer, as I did, and they were always busy at the school. The school bus picked them up and delivered them right at our driveway.

One of the finest additions to our family was when I bought a golden retriever pup that we called Brutus. He was the most intelligent animal and friend to my family that I have ever had. My kids loved him and he would play and retrieve for them all day long in the river or on the lawn. When I dropped the kids off up river a couple miles with their inner tubes, Brutus would swim down river with them until they all got to the ranch. If I wanted my kids home after they had taken the ATV across the river and some miles into the woods, I would point and tell Brutus to go and get the kids. When Brutus showed up, my children knew I had sent him, and I wanted them home. If a fox happened to get loose on the ranch, Brutus would chase him towards me and I would scoop up the fox with a net on a pole. Foxes always ran the edge of the guard fence and they were very fast. Brutus went everywhere with me. We had his companionship for nearly fourteen years. I wanted, but never got another dog.

On one beautiful spring day, I took Brutus for a walk down the ranch road to the river where the ice was starting to break up. As we walked down, Brutus wanted me to throw his stick for him that he had in his mouth. I did a few times and as we walked past the pond that was still frozen over, I threw his stick onto the ice a fair distance. I did not realize that part of the pond ice was getting thin. Brutus went through near the middle of the pond. With his stick in his mouth he struggled to climb out and onto the ice. His thick coat was heavy with water as he tried time after time to climb out of the water onto the ice. He went around and around trying to get himself out all around of this hole he had made. I kept encouraging him and he gave a great effort, but to no avail. After a long while of him thrashing around, I heard him starting to choke and I could see he was tiring.

I ran to the side of the pond that I knew to be only three or four feet deep and took off my boots, coat and jeans. With only socks, underwear and a T-shirt on, I stepped onto the ice. About my third or fourth step I too broke through, very refreshing to say the least. With my feet on the bottom I started to smash the ice in front of me with my forearms, making slow progress towards Brutus who I could now tell was only a few more seconds away from drowning. I could not feel my arms anymore, but I kept smashing through. By the time I reached the hole where he was, he had gone under. I felt around under the water for him. The first thing I felt was his stupid stick that he still had in his mouth. I pulled him to the surface with the stick in one hand and a handful of fur in my other. He took a few breaths, coughing and sputtering. I pushed him ahead of me through the trail of broken ice that I had made. I went to push him towards shore again but both my feet were stuck in the mud. I worked them free and kept pushing him ahead.

He was able to swim a little now through the ice. I finally, with one more big push, got him where he could get himself out. He must have brought up a gallon of water that was in his stomach once on shore. But now I was worried about me. I could not feel a thing as hyperthermia had set in for sure. I left Brutus and my clothes behind and ran as fast as I could to the house. As soon as I got to the house, I was in the shower in seconds. Not able to feel anything, I was worried about how hot the water was. I might scald myself and not even feel it. So I made sure I had the cold water on halfway with the hot. I am not sure who else was home but I told them to go and check on Brutus and get him into the house and help him dry off.

I stayed in the shower until all the hot water was used up. Only after getting out of the shower did I notice that my forearms were cut to ribbons from breaking the ice with them. I managed to bandage my arms and I put the warmest clothes that I could find on. Drank some hot coffee with lots of rum.

IAN COBB

Brutus.

Jeffrey and Dad floating, while the others played in the river behind the ranch.

Graham and I having a ride at home.

IAN COBB

Graham, Jeffery and Lisa, safely back from a ride on the ATV.

The kids told me later that Brutus had made his way back to the house and was still carrying that stupid stick. They dried him off and covered him up with an old blanket. Next day he was fine, but I was hurting big time, but okay.

Many years later living in Ontario, it became that time that every dog owner dreads. I had to put this great dog down. I made sure the kids were in school. Brutus was lying down in a lot of pain when I administered the injection and he drifted off into dog heaven. It was a very tough day. I never got another dog.

When I first started to raise foxes in 1975, there were only 8000 ranched fox pelts on the market, world wide. By 1992 there were 8,000,000 fox pelts for sale in the auction houses of the world. The price dropped big time from a high of $300 or $500 per pelt to a low of about

$50. That was not even enough to cover the cost of feed for other farmers around the globe. But for me, I was still making good money, with my cost at around $13 to produce each pelt. But I knew this day would come. After all I was selling breeding stock around the world for $1000 each. And every fox that I sold was producing more. I knew there was going to be a day of reckoning because of overproduction. But I had prepared for this day. I now had two choices.

The first was that I could continue to work like a dog seven days a week and still make money even though my accountant told me that I would never have to work a day in my life again. Or I could sell all my foxes, alive, to a foreign buyer who had approached me six months earlier.

I also had my growing family's future to think about now. I thought it might be time to get my family out of the woods of New Brunswick and back to the economy in central Canada, now that I had made enough to purchase a home, a small store or business and take care of all our needs including a university education for all the kids And to maybe salvage my marriage that was in trouble; love and romance had taken a back seat in order to make every cent that I could out of this industry before it would crash as I knew it was going to from global overproduction. I knew this was a cyclical market when I went into it. And I was getting out on the next downturn.

Halfway before the downturn in the fur market, two Chinese businessmen had come to my fox ranch and wanted to purchase every breeder that I would sell them. I had told them that I was getting $1000 each for them in past years and they told me that price was a little rich for them and they left my ranch.

Two years later, I made a decision that I would now sell out. I contacted the Chinese and they were still eager to get every fox that I could get my hands on. We came to an agreement of $75 for every fox. I put the word out that I would buy everyone's foxes for $50 each if delivered to my ranch. That was as much or more money than what they were going to get after all the work of pelting and waiting for their fur checks. Every pen on my ranch was full to capacity with foxes from everywhere.

The Chinese used a broker to set up all the transportation. There was no protocol between Canada and Communist China for this kind of transaction. So this concerned me when clearing their check through the bank. They ordered two tractor trailer cattle trucks that showed up at my ranch. We loaded hundreds of cages of foxes on them. It was the wee hours of the night when we had finished loading. Now all I needed was confirmation from my bank manager in Vancouver, telling me that the check drawn on the Bank of Hong Kong had cleared before I allowed the trucks to pull out of my ranch. When I got the call that the check had cleared, I told the drivers they could head out to the USA border and the Bangor, Maine airport, where there was a 747 plane waiting to fly direct to China. Feed and water went with them as well. The foxes were in transit and did not have to be quarantined.

I sold and got rid of all animals on my farm and next started to dismantle the ranch. I was never going to be able to sell the house and barn with all these wire pens and sheds on the property. I first sold all my tools and equipment. Next I took out an advertisement in every newspaper in New Brunswick, P.E.I. and Nova Scotia that I was holding an auction on my farm for all my used wire, steel roofing and rough lumber. That Saturday morning there was a lineup of trucks at my farm. I personally auctioned off every stick of wood and every piece of guard fence, wire and pens for cash and they had two weeks to take it down and remove it. It was a great success.

Next I got a government grant to put the land back to reusable green belt farm land. I hired a backhoe to dig a hole and a dozer to push all the leftover junk into, and I leveled the field and seeded with timothy and clover, before putting a for sale sign on the front lawn.

I decided to now rent a motor home and take the family to Ontario to check out which town or city we might like to move to. We checked out Kingston, Ontario first. Next we looked around Picton where my brother lives. Picton is on a peninsula that protrudes out in Lake Ontario forty-five miles.

We looked around different other cities along the north shore of Lake Ontario, settling on Belleville. It is of the 401 highway, halfway between Montreal and Toronto and an easy drive to Ottawa as well.

We continued our vacation slowly driving the motor home to Niagara Falls and headed back to New Brunswick by way of the USA south side of Lake Ontario.

Over that summer I did not have any bites on selling the house and barn, so before school started in the fall, I flew the family to Disney in Florida.

Once back home, I told Dawn that I was going to have to find something to do until we sold the place. She spotted a sales job that might work for me. A new company was opening up an office in Moncton, selling gourmet frozen food. They were looking for ten salespeople to sell door to door. They supplied a small brand new truck with a freezer on back. So first thing Monday morning I headed into Moncton, to discover a line of potential sales candidates stretching from the strip mall doorway to around the corner of the block. I parked my car and walked right passed everyone in line and through the doorway. I saw a fella standing on a chair, handing out applications and giving information. Just then a door opened and a potential candidate came out from an office. I motioned to this fellow that was standing on the chair and I got his attention. I shouted to him that he wanted to speak to me and I pointed to the open door. He yelled back to me. "Who?", "Mike?"

"Yes", I said "Mike wants to talk to me."

He beckoned to me and I squeezed my way past others and went into the office saying to the fellow sitting at the desk, Hi Mike, I was told you wanted to speak to me. He asked me to close the door. He told me I needed a $500 deposit down for a new truck and product to sell. I said it was not a problem, but I wanted to see the product first that I would be selling. The minute I saw it, I told him that it looked great; I was going to be able to sell a lot for him. He called in one of his trainers into the office and we went out on the road to see how the pitch was played selling this product. Everything was frozen and well displayed and packed in boxes. The freezer on the truck could hold fifty to fifty-five boxes. There were all kinds of fantastic cuts of steak, many different gourmet stuffed chicken, fish, lobster, scallops, and all kinds of food. Even pizza sticks and cheesecakes to mention a few. I would make $20 for every box that I sold. Each morning I would pay the secretary for what I had sold the day before and I would load up with more.

I had a great time doing this job. I sold a lot of product. It was a new product to the area and a lot of people wanted to try it. After a few weeks I started to go to small businesses and tell the owners that they could write it off as an expense for entertainment. Their check was their receipt. It was not long before I was selling 50% of the stock of the office. I was making between $300 and a $1000 per day clear. Where was this job when I needed one years ago? So here I was again, making hay when the sun shines, sometimes working seven days a week. They gave me a small plaque as the first salesperson to sell a hundred boxes in a week in the Moncton office. I loved this job.

My son Graham at ten years old would come with me on Saturdays and I showed him how to sell. I even had him put on a training sales pitch to the whole office a couple of times. Every salesperson had to do a demo in front of the rest of the sales team a couple of times. Graham made money to help pay for his hockey goaltender equipment.

Most of the other sales people stayed working the streets in and around Moncton. But I would cover a different city each week and I kept a record of each person and business that bought from me. I would revisit them every four or five weeks. I built up a fantastic customer base, mostly small businesses.

Once, working in Fredericton, I walked into the provincial government building. I was carrying five boxes of my best sellers, including lobster. I asked to see the Premier who at the time was the Honorable Frank McKenna. Do you have an appointment, asked the guard inside the building? No, I said, I am just bringing the Premier his lobster. I was told which was his office and I walked in. His secretary, sitting at her desk, asked me the same question, what is your name and do you have an appointment? This time I answered, yes, I have his lobster here. She told me to have a seat and she got up, opened the large door to the Premier's office and entered, closing the door behind her. I got up with my boxes and opened the door and walked in.

The secretary was telling me, you can't come in here, and I pretended to be struggling carrying the boxes as I kept walking towards the Premier's desk. Putting them down on the corner of his large desk I said to the secretary, loud enough for the Premier to hear me, that I did not want his lobster to spoil. He was on the phone at the time and motioned to his secretary that it was okay and she left the room. He was on the phone for about two or three more minutes, then turned to me saying, "What lobster?" I opened the first box and showed him. Nice, he said. I opened up the next box of bacon wrapped filet mignon. After showing him all five different products, I told him that I had sixty more boxes outside on my truck for him to look at. He said, just a moment, picked up the phone and called his wife at home. He asked her if the large 22 cubic foot freezer in the garage was plugged in yet. He gave me the address of his home and I was there in half an hour. After going through them all with his wife, she gave me a check for fifty-two of my sixty boxes, about $2650. That was my second largest sale to one person. That sales performance sure empowered me to try all kinds of different ways to display my products. I just loved the challenge in making the sale, and the products were all gourmet quality.

I used the same pitch at the RCMP headquarters in Fredericton; I had to talk to a box telling them that I had their commander's lobster delivery in my truck. On the speaker they told me the commander's name, and they raised the entrance gate to the fortified underground that I drove down into. It was a heavily guarded large area under the building. There were uniform and non-uniform personnel walking all over the area. I was told their boss would be down to see me in about 20 minutes; he was in a meeting. I asked a few headquarters personnel how it was that their boss was getting lobster and steaks and not them. A few stopped and I put on a show for them sitting on the back corner of the box of my truck. I sold about eight boxes to them before the commander showed up. I reversed my statement to him saying that I was glad he showed up before all the others bought all of his lobster. I think he bought six boxes. I'll remember that sale all my life. It was so much fun!

Salisbury and New Brunswick were very good to me and my family. I contributed back to their economy as well. I had done my things and been successful. Time to move on. The village sign says it all—Salisbury, Home of the Silver Fox.

In the spring I received my first and only offer for my property and I took it. I did not need the cash so I took 50% of his mortgage at a very nice interest rate for five years. The closing date was after the kids finished the school year.

The house that I had bought so long ago had been vastly changed by all my years of renovations. It had been hard work, but making it energy efficient had been one of the best investments I had ever made. We left this house in 1993.

I loved my time in New Brunswick. This province had been very good to us. The area we lived in was fantastic area and so were the people of the province. But when the fur industry hit a time of overproduction, it was time to return to central Canada. This busy working seven days a week, learning new methods on the job, trying to be a success, took its toll on my marriage.

It was time to move on.

My wife never wanted to be a farmer's wife in the first place. She was a trooper and pitched in at most everything to help. But the love and romance we had was at an end.

CHAPTER
14
Finding My Place in Belleville

I drove back to Belleville, Ontario to find a home close to good schools and where the kids would now experience living in a city, biking on streets, newspaper routes, hockey and baseball. I also coached both sports. I also wanted closer access to the Montreal Canadiens hockey games in Montreal, my second entertainment passion in life.

I checked out other things such as being on the west side of the prevailing winds to avoid breathing the city

Chris Malette, City Editor, 962-9171, ext. 229

INTELLIGENCER PHOTO BY DARKO ZELJKOV

Proud of his pigeons

Ian Cobb, who has raced pigeons since age 12, looks with pride at one of his racing pigeons at his Village Drive home. Cobb, who belongs to Kingston's Lime Stone City Fliers Club was preparing to take several of his one-year-old racing pigeons for a 320-kilometre race this wekend.

I have raced pigeons since I was eight years old.
Here is one of my Belleville racers from my last flock.

pollutions. I talked to the police department to discover where the area of town was that they had the least calls of complaints from.

I also needed a large back yard to race my homing pigeons from. There were a lot of great flyers around this area and I was going to have a lot of fun with them.

I found a great spot for us in Belleville, a large four-bedroom two-bathroom home with a very large back yard. I had a large in-ground swimming pool installed as well.

I felt a little sorry for my son Jeffrey, who was always a top student in New Brunswick. He was going into his last year of high school and now would not be able to graduate with all the other kids that he had started school with in grade one. So I went to the Salisbury school and spoke to the high school principal and we struck a deal. If I would have the principal of the high school in Belleville send Jeffrey's marks to him at mid-term, if they were good enough he could graduate from Salisbury High School. His marks were great and I flew Jeffrey to Salisbury to graduate with his friends. Jeffrey now has two high school graduation diplomas from two provinces.

I told him that he was the first Cobb to ever graduate high school and that I had never even graduated from elementary school. He went on to take business at Carleton University in Ottawa and later Policing at Loyalist College. He has worked at a number of jobs including as a customs broker for private industry and now for Canada Post.

I had promised my wife that once we got to Ontario I would buy a small store so that she would have a job and something to do. She had mostly worked outside of the home and was not your average stay-at-home person. So we bought a pet food retail franchise that the whole family chipped in to run. My wife worked hard at it. My daughter Shannon had left Toronto and returned to Calgary a few years earlier. Things were not going as she had planned out west. So I offered her a job at our pet food store which she accepted and moved into the house with us. Shannon was a good worker and got along well with Dawn at the store.

After being in Belleville for a few weeks I received a call from the owner of Meridian Foods head office in Toronto wanting to come to Belleville to meet with me. He had a proposition for me. At that meeting he wanted to know if I would entertain the idea of me opening an office for them in Kingston, Ontario. I told them I was not interested in driving forty-five minutes to work and back each day. So they asked If I thought I could manage an office for them in Belleville and service cities from Ottawa, Kingston to Oshawa, which is a huge territory. I told them I could handle that for them. So we spent a few days looking for an office location in Belleville.

We found one and they built two offices, a huge walk-in freezer and warehouse. They gave me ten brand new trucks and two trainers and hired a secretary for me. We interviewed and hired ten salespersons. With the two trainers and myself, we trained all of my sales team. I told them that they had to put their own personalities into doing this job and that it was not going to be for all of them. I soon realized that most of the people were not willing to put in the effort that was needed daily to be successful. I had to phone some of them at home to see if they were coming into work that day. Some of them stole product and said that they were robbed. Another guy drove one of my trucks to Calgary. The police found it there abandoned, with all the product gone as well. After one year, I had had enough of trying to motivate lazy people and I resigned. They brought in a manager from some other location and after six months the office closed its doors.

I made a deal with my children, that after they graduated with a diploma from high school, I would buy them their first car if they had the ability to pay their own insurance and maintenance to operate it. Jeffrey wanted a brand new V.W. and he paid for a lot of it with his hard-earned savings after graduating from college. Graham wanted a truck and I bought him one once he had a job. Even though my daughter Lisa never produced a diploma from high school or college, she was a single mother and needed a car which I bought for her.

Secondly if they wanted to go to university or college, I would pay in full for all their years of attendance provided they showed me a graduation diploma first. But I was not paying for a party! And thirdly, when it came time to buy their first home, I would help with the down payment, provided they showed me that they were debt-free.

I wanted to support them but after a life of hard work, I also wanted them to understand the value of effort.

Once the children had moved out on their own, I knew my marriage was over. My wife was not a happy camper living here in Ontario. Our marriage had been in trouble for years. With the love and romance gone, we both drifted apart on many fronts and it became just too frustrating for both of us to continue on. I lacked the patience and was to blame for a lot of discontent. I had lived and worked all my life in a very different building than most people. I was always looking for the next adventure, and I often needed and asked for her help to compensate for my own deficiencies which I never explained to her. And it was always my suggestions and my adventures, never our adventures. I did not consult her or consider how she might have wanted a different life.

Throughout our marriage, most things had to be done my way because I saw myself as the only one putting any thought or planning into it. I had difficulty in understanding other ways of achieving; I only knew my way.

Dawn had started to drink heavily, probably out of stress and frustration. And I believe now I was the cause of much

Holding my owl.

of that stress, that I was probably responsible for her drinking. She began to have seizures. With no hope for things getting better, we just decided to divorce. She went back to her family in New Brunswick.

It was a sad time, and I still miss her today, for how she helped me, but I was too much of a burden for her, and I often reacted with a lot of disrespect and anger. And I was turning into someone that I did not understand or like as well either.

I had meetings with doctors and psychiatrists because of my erratic behavior and I was assessed and diagnosed with post traumatic stress from severe concussions years earlier and my very stressful past life, going all the way back to my abusive childhood from detentions, strappings and beatings at school and home. Mental health is not something you go around sharing, so I have never spoken of it to anyone but my doctor. Until now.

Now that we were living in Ontario I got involved with the local Ontario Hockey League Major Junior A Belleville Bulls hockey team, as a fan as well as billeting some of their players in my home. It was great hockey played here by a lot of young men that went on to having good careers in and out of the game. Each Friday night that the team was not on the road, I would make a huge spaghetti with my special sauce for the whole team. All the boys were going to high school. Some of the older boys did university correspondence. Each day after high school they would go to the rink for practice. I would go and watch them. All my children played hockey and ringette as well. I would also go on scouting trips around the OHL with pro scout Connie Broden who was scouting for the Winnipeg Jets at that time. He was the first guy I told I could not read or write, but asked him not to tell anyone.

At home I cooked supper most nights and I did the shopping. My grocery bill took a large increase with such an active household. After supper everyone did homework and just hung out, watching TV or just relaxing. I was a friend and a second parent for them. They were all between sixteen and twenty years of age. A lot of them went on to play in the National Hockey League or worked for other professional and amateur teams around the world. Some are still in the game today as coaches. One of my favorite young players to live with my family while playing junior hockey was James Boyd, who has gone on in the game to now be the General Manager of the Ottawa 67s, of the OHL and who took them to the Memorial Cup. Many former players stay in touch with me today. I had the great pleasure and fun to billet and feed some fantastic young men at our home in Belleville.

One of the first things that I did when moving to Belleville was to build a new racing pigeon loft and moved my birds into their new home. Being homing pigeons, I could not let them out of the loft or they would head back to New Brunswick. So these pigeons were only used to breed and raise young. I had three lofts in the one main loft building. One was for the breeders that had nest boxes with an exterior fly pen at the end of the main loft so they could go out and sunbathe. The middle of the loft was for my youngsters with just about a hundred perches and this is where my youngsters were trained to home to and race to during the young bird races in late summer. The third section was for my adult racing team with their nest boxes. I had a great time racing them with a lot of different clubs in our area.

Years later, a medical university in my area was doing research on Parkinson's, Alzheimer's and dementia and wanted to purchase my whole loft of birds. Apparently these diseases are being spawned from an area of our brain that humans no longer have to use. It is the navigational part of our brain where the cells are no longer needed to be turned on anymore. The Australians were also working with a highly navigational specie of bird, the albatross. Both universities were trying to do similar research. I wanted to be free to do some traveling and after having pigeons for nearly sixty years, I told the university that I would sell my whole loft to them. There was one condition: that I be involved in the research as the handler and I helped build their loft and I took them and flew them over different terrain for them. They planted chips into their brains, attached mini cameras and GPS devices to them. I would even fly the birds over huge iron ore deposits. All this information was downloaded into their computer along with dozens of other experiments. After some time I offered some of my findings that I had discovered when doing concussion research on the foxes in New Brunswick.

Today researchers have discovered the protein to be able to turn on these brain cells of our former dormant navigation neurons. They have even discovered how to completely reverse Alzheimer's in animals in less than thirty days. The war continues with the large pharmaceutical corporations opposing research on humans. Big Pharma is simply making too much profit off these diseases.

With Dawn and the children gone, I was now living alone in a large Belleville four-bedroom home, and I advertised and interviewed for a quality boarder. One person who moved into the house was a transferring postie named Jim. He was originally from Cape Breton and had worked for the post office for many years in Ontario. He was your typical Maritimer, happy, honest and hard-working. He boarded here on two different occasions for a couple years before getting his own place. Jim likes the ladies, but he is a confirmed bachelor for whatever reason. We have become very good friends. We have phoned or visited each other a few times each week to talk sports and stuff for the past sixteen years or so. I had taken a few other boarders over the years as well.

My home in Belleville which I now share with Andrée.

I could not just sit on my hands, so I started to drive a school bus for a few years. I soon learned that the different school bus companies were treating all their drivers very poorly. So I took it upon myself to try to change things for the better for the drivers. I decided to find some representation for them. I spoke to the leader of the NDP, Jack Layton, in Ottawa. I asked him who might be a good union fit for what I had in mind to do. Here I am an entrepreneur business fellow talking to a socialist. But it was a great move. He gave me a list of people and unions to call and interview. After some consultation I decided to hire the Teamster Union. And did I ever pick the best professional persons to form a bus drivers union for us.

We unionized and signed contracts with five bus companies for about 450 bus drivers. I then got out of the bus driving racket as I was a marked man. I did it for others who were not in a position to stand up to the corruption or were not as independent monetarily as I was.

Unhappy with how bus drivers were being treated,
I spearheaded an effort to unionize bus drivers.

As you can probably tell by now, I want and need to be around people. And I was lonely. It was February 13th, 1998, my birthday that I attended a Belleville Bulls hockey game. I had no one to celebrate my birthday with and wanted to find somewhere to go after the game. I remember seeing a singles dance sign at the Belleville Legion. So I went to check it out and ended up having a fantastic time. Good music and a lot of single ladies to dance with from a lot of different cities who came each week to these dances.

IAN COBB

I met a great-looking former school teacher named Joy, living in Peterborough, and danced most of the night with her. At the end of the night she asked if I was coming to next week's dance, and I said I would.

It was the fourth week of dances that Joy and her friend who always came together told me that they were going to Cuba to a wedding of a family member who lived in Nova Scotia. Joy's girlfriend had a boyfriend that I met at the dances, but Joy asked me if I would be interested in going to Cuba with her. I jumped at the chance and we started to date and hang out for the next four years or so. She even moved in with me for six months or so when she wanted to move back to her hometown area where her two daughters lived ten miles north of Belleville. She moved out of my home once she had found a place in her hometown to be close to her two daughters and their families. I was disappointed but that is what she had always told me; she wanted to be closer to her grandkids.

So it was back to the single dances for me. I got to know some nice ladies at these dances and I even took one of them for a trip to New Orleans to Mardi Gras. Just something I always wanted to do. But I could not drive back home fast enough to drop off my traveling partner. I became much more selective meeting with the ladies for sure after that.

I had met another gal, a quieter, non-smoking non-drinking lady from the Eastern Township of Quebec, Andrée, who lived and had raised her family in Kingston right out of high school and was now divorced. She had just purchased a small older home in Kingston. We enjoyed dancing together and she did not carry a lot of personal baggage with her. There was no pressure from either one of us. We just started hanging out with each other for company. We had a few things in common. Mostly sports and dancing.

For a time, I sold produce from a farm truck. And Andrée decided to help me. We made a great team.

About that time I needed something to do and I answered an ad for someone to drive a five-ton truck from a farm in Prince Edward County each day to Kingston. We parked at the large Canadian Tire store parking lot there, and sold produce grown on this wonderful farmer's huge operation. He grew everything, many varieties of berries, all of the vegetables, and fruit grown throughout the whole growing seasons, from early spring to the pumpkins in late autumn. I set up signs, tables and umbrellas each morning and displayed all the produce for sale. This truck would average selling about $500 to $600 of produce seven days a week for the past few years. It was not too long before I had the sales up to $1600 to $2000 per day. They were long days but I just loved it.

Andrée started to show up at the truck each morning to help me out. It was not very far for her to drive. She would hop up in the truck and make up baskets of beans, berries, potatoes, apples and everything else, so all I had to do was put it onto the table and it freed me up in order to sell. I called people over to the truck and walked them down the table showing all that I had for sale. I even went over to tourists in their motor homes that came into the parking lot and asked if they had a refrigerator in their vehicle that needed filling.

People would come to the stand and ask for a dozen sweet corn, but I would tell them that I could not sell them any corn. Even though they could see many bags of corn in the truck, I would say, come over here, and they would, and I would walk them to all the rest of the produce and ask them if they could use some of this one or the other as I walked them down the length of the display. After I could not sell them more, I told them that the reason I could not sell them corn was because the corn was so good it sold itself. Instead of just selling some of the sweetest corn in the country, they left with $50 or more of my other produce.

I found so many different ways to sell that I would just crack myself up. Andrée used to laugh so hard at some of my antics she would wet her pants more than once laughing. It was a great way to make good money, be out in the public and be productive at something, and at the same time having great days with my new friend Andrée. We did have a lot of fun!

That fall and winter Andrée was having some problems with her home in Kingston, first her hot water tank blew up and flooded the basement so badly that the fire department had to show up to help. Maintaining the older house became a large chore for her. She had a small apartment with a student boarder in the basement, and things were not going smoothly with this fellow. Andrée did not smoke and did not want smoking in her home. Next the basement wall sprung a leak in the spring and the whole basement floor had a few inches of water. Things were getting a bit much for her to deal with. Her hands are very crippled up from rheumatoid arthritis that is also affecting other parts of her body. She is on very heavy medication. So I made her an offer to help her sell her house and move in with me as I had a very large four- bedroom empty house. So some months later she sold her house and we moved her into mine. She took over two of the bedrooms upstairs, we share the main floor and I have a master bedroom and bathroom in the basement where I have always stayed.

In the spring, the farmer that I had worked for the previous year called me and wanted to know if I was going to work on the same truck again this year for him. I said yes I would, and I asked Andrée if she wanted to help me out with it again, since we had so much fun last year. And yes, she was up for it again. We had a very fun time and some crazy memories doing this job that spring summer and fall.

After some months of both of us having a pretty good time working and going places together, I held a house party with a lot of our friends that we had made over a couple years.

Before this party I put an ad in the paper, wanting to purchase a special ring for me to give Andree as an engagement ring. And I bought a beauty ring to give her.

During the party I went down on one knee just like in the movies and asked her to marry me. She said

I decided to ask Andrée to marry me.
Here is my ad looking for the very special ring I wanted.

yes and I put this very substantial diamond ring on her finger. And I thought I would be able to have a full and loving relationship with a wife. But she gave the ring back to me a couple days later, saying that once married was enough for her. And that was that. We just stayed good friends sharing the expenses and duties of running my home and we continued to watch our sports and go dancing together at different locations in our area. She lives upstairs in my home and I live downstairs. I do the shopping and cooking and Andree does the laundry and keeps the house ship shape. A different relationship for sure, but it seems to have worked for the past thirteen years.

When Andrée first moved into my home she also brought a computer with her and encouraged me to try to learn how to read and write on it. The first thing that I noticed was that the letters did not dance and merge on the computer screen like they do for me on paper. And that the lines did not merge and become blurry like they did for me reading on paper in a book. It took months of learning how to spell enough words to make a sentence that was not all red from misspelling on the computer screen. I drove Andree crazy asking her how to spell this and that to create one sentence at a time. I learned how to use spell check, and that was such a tool for me.

I found a hockey site called Habs Inside Out, HIO for short. It has since been changed to Hockey Inside Out, because of infringement rights of a corporate logo. This was the site that I stayed on for about eight hours a day reading. Many months later I posted my very first writings in my life in a post explaining that at this late time of my life, this post was my

Behind this HIO door of my room is where I learned how to read and write on computer in 2006.

IAN COBB

Béliveau photo and message both sides. This photo was given to me signed by Jean Béliveau at our 4th HIO Summit. He then asked me if I knew who took this picture. I said I did not know. He told me that I took this picture, when I was doing odd jobs around the Montreal Forum as a teenager and he wanted me to have it.

IAN COBB
63 Village DR.
BELLEVILLE ONTARIO
K8P 4K2

IAN GRANT COBB
63 VILLAGE DR
BELLEVILLE ON
K8P 4K2

maintenar

NOTE: Both S
in qua
on the

Phil Goyette
Jacque Plante
#15 Marcel Bonin
19 ALBERT JR. Langlois
Tom Johnson
Doug HARVEY
Ralph BACKSTROM
Donnie Marshall
Dickie Moore
JEAN Beliveau
AB McDonald
Bob Turner
ANDRE PRONOVOST
JEAN Guy Talbot
Billy HICKEY
GEOFFRION (BERNIE Boom Boom)
HENRI Richard - (HIDDEN behind Don MARshall)

FRANK SELKIE
TOE BLAKE (HECTOR)

1958-59
Montreal Canadiens

Given to Ian as a remembrance for his help around the Forum with the TEAM for 3yrs. as a kid. in the late 50's by Jean Beliveau
2010 - 100th yr. celibration

Names of players featured in photo.
The Pocket Rocket is behind Don Marshall.

first time communicating by reading and writing. Mostly Habs fans on the site responded to my post and each day would help me to write properly. Andree and sport writers Mike Boone, Dave Stubbs and Pat Hickey were the people most responsible for me being a literary genius today. Along with all of the HIO fans that used to come on the HIO site helping me with proper language each and every day for two years.

In pay back for their gift of helping me to become literate, I became very involved in the HIO summit as a charity event since our first group summit get together in 2007, with a HIO poster who wanted to meet in Montreal and go to a game at the Bell Center. Here is part of an article written by a HIO poster about how HIO came into being and how a few of the HIO members came to Montreal to meet up for a game. I just could not let this summit event die. So I picked up the ball the following year and we have grown this into an annual charity event.

Here is part of a synopsis about our very first HIO fan charity Summit, written by Robert Lefevre.

Damn, did we all have a good time!

Super sized kudos to Jason Weiss (Jay in PA) for spearheading an evening that will long be remembered by all of those who took part in the day's activities. I'm sure that I speak for everyone in saying that this man is a class act for endeavoring to take on the task of coordinating much of what went on.

Jay, who lives in Pittsburgh, had lots of long distance help from J.T., Naila, Jim M, Sami, Kullkullan and Manapart in setting things up from ticket orders to the final gathering at Hurley's Pub. I hope that my documenting of the day does their hard work justice.

I personally had a blast meeting up with everyone. It is 4 AM after the game, as I begin to post this, having just arrived home and editing roughly 70 photographs taken during the day.

Remembering the names of everyone (after meeting close to 40 of you) gets a little hazy. Posting this entry will have taken up my entire Sunday by the time it is finished.

I try to not post long thoughts and ramblings at Habs Inside Out for the most part, I tend to merely weigh in on the subject at hand and offer my larger thoughts through a link for those curious enough to enjoy. It was so gratifying for me to associate faces with names and see in person.

Throughout the day and the evening, I felt friendships and kinships being born, and I will truly miss a bunch of you until we do this all again.

The icing on my cake was rubbing elbows with Dave Stubbs, Mike Boone, Kevin Mio and Pat Hickey. Habs Inside Out is Dave's baby, and it warmed me to see him looking at the gathering so proudly. The evening was his community coming to fruition. Dave's creation and hard work resulted in an evening such as this, and it is a credit to the man's imagination and positiveness of spirit that he jumped on the idea of a Habs Fans Summit within hours of it being suggested. Thanks so much for running with it, Mr. Stubbs!

After this first get-together in 2007 and for the past thirteen years now, I have organized and brought all these wonderful fans and now friends with their families to Montreal from all

The very first HIO Fan Charity Summit. Great times, great people!

over the globe for this full weekend of events at our HIO FAN CHARITY HOCKEY SUMMIT, I have made this weekend event into a great time for Habs fans to get together as well as a charity fundraiser for the Montreal Canadiens Children's Foundation. We now have fans that come from all across North America, Europe, Asia, and Australia. These fans over the years have become wonderful friends to one another and are like my family. Here is Mike Boone's story on me, published in *The Montreal Gazette*.

Mike Boone's story on Ian Cobb appeared in Hockey Inside/Out, published today in *The Gazette*:

> *This is the heartwarming story of a former dead-end kid who found friendship and happiness on the Internet.*
>
> *No, Ian Cobb's favourite site isn't kinky.*
>
> *It's hockey.*

Cobb is a resident of Belleville, Ont., who has spent most of his 65 years concealing a secret. He couldn't read or write. About 18 months ago, he discovered Habs Inside/Out, where the words began to make sense because Cobb cared about what Dave Stubbs, Pat Hickey and I were writing.

We're not making outlandish claims here. The Gazette's Canadiens fansite can't bring eyesight to the blind. It can't cure cancer.

But Habs Inside/Out helped Ian Cobb. And he's given back by posting countless comments and by becoming the primary organizer of the second annual Habs Inside/Out Summit, which brought about 80 fans to the Bell Centre for the Oct. 25 game against Anaheim. The Canadiens lost that night, but Cobb's enthusiasm was undiminished. A typical post: "Boys and girls! We don't need anyone to tell us that we have a shot at the Cup this year. We, the most perceptive and most informative hockey fans in the world, have been treated and shown how this game is to be played and won for 100 years. We recognize quality and expect performance, from management to throughout the organization ..."

Here's how Cobb describes himself in his Habs Inside/Out profile: "Born in Montreal ... Worked many different jobs around Montreal. As a kid, later went working pipeline construction as a labourer, equipment operator and scuba diver for oil & gas co's ... owned and operated two corporations in three provinces, illiterate until my 60s. Raised three children, retired 10 years ago as just your average millionaire, drive school bus and read and write on Inside/Out, learning here every day with friends!!!" That's the bare-bones outline. As he's told me over too many beers at Habs I/O Summits I and II and in a phone conversation last week, Cobb has done a lot of living since his youth in South Shore St. Lambert.

"My dad was a welder, a church-going man and all that kind of stuff," Cobb recalls. "He didn't know why his son couldn't read or write.

"I felt I let the family down.

I walked around with different inferiority complexes, pissed the bed till I was 12. I was scared to go to school and got strapped every day." Neither his father nor his teachers knew that Cobb was Dyslexic and partly deaf. In the absence of a diagnosis and special-needs instruction, he stumbled along, repeating Grades 5 and 6.

"I got to know everyone in high school," Cobb recalls, "because they all went by me." He dropped out without finishing elementary school. Cobb was illiterate, but "I could bulls— with the best of them, and I learned how to do that." How good was Cobb at concealing his disability? "My wife of 30 years never knew I couldn't read or write," he says.

But, as Cobb's posted CV indicates, he could do a variety of jobs that didn't require literacy. He was a teenager, washing dishes at a restaurant near the Forum, when Danny Gallivan took a shine to him and set up Cobb with a room at the downtown YMCA and various oddjobs around the Forum.

"Boom-Boom Geoffrion had a big blue station wagon," Cobb recalls, "and I used to start it up for *him on cold days." While living at the Y, Cobb would hang out at the Sir George Williams University library in the adjoining building on Drummond St. He couldn't read the books, but he liked to look at the pictures.*

Fiercely proud of "never taking a friggin' handout in my life," Cobb reels off a long list of work experiences that took him from the dress-alteration department at Sears to pipeline construction in Alberta and Kentucky to a jail cell in Oregon (it's a long story, involving papers that were not in order).

"I'd go with the flow," Cobb says. "My first trip out west was riding the freight cars." The constant was Cobb's ability to live by his wits, without benefit of the alphabet. He didn't have to be literate to run a ranch in New Brunswick, where Cobb had 2,000 silver foxes and 36,000 minks in P.E.I, breeding animals to supply furriers on Mayor St. in Montreal and developing a feed formula he sold to Ralston Purina. He was the first to artificially inseminate wild animals.

Another constant: passion for hockey. Since moving to Belleville in 1993, Cobb was billeting Belleville junior hockey players and had team spaghetti dinners in his home each week with players such as James Boyd, (whom is GM of the Ottawa 67's today) Craig Mills, Dan Cleary, Jonathan Cheechoo and many more – for the Ontario Hockey League's Belleville Bulls.

Cobb is living with a woman, Andrée, who had a computer and helped him with dyslexia and following the Canadiens at a distance when he stumbled on Habs. Inside/Out.

"My first post to the site, I didn't even know how to use Spell Check," he says.

There have been maybe 500 posts since – all knowledgeable, none a literary classic.

"I'd get up in the morning and go on Habs Inside/out," he says, "and I didn't know how to go on another site. I had a dictionary, my friend Andrée and everybody on the HIO site giving me help.

"I didn't have to look anyone in the eye and feel my face go red every time I screwed up a word. It was so exciting to be able to communicate.

"I learned to read and write on Habs Inside/out. There's no doubt about it."

Ian celebrating in the Montreal Canadiens media room.

I met a great many people through this HIO hockey site that have helped me with my reading and writing skills and they have become my friends. And the charity event has grown tremendously. Each year we have between one hundred and two hundred people, who are now friends, coming to this weekend charity event from all over the globe, including Australia.

Over these years I have had fantastic support from *The Montreal Gazette* newspaper staff, The Montreal Canadiens Hockey Club and our wonderful Hockey Inside Out members who have become a family of friends to me. These people are a large part of my life as we communicate online daily with each other and gather each year in Montreal. (You can view stories and pictures of these past 13 years on my "*Montreal Canadiens We Are Fans Summit*") Facebook site.

— Montreal Canadiens We Are Fans Summit

Some of these fine people even stop by Belleville and have a drink with me around my pool when travelling up or down the highway from all over North America when on vacation et cetera. The one common denominator that binds us together is, of course, hockey. A lot of us think we are great hockey General Managers, but mostly we have become wonderful friends. Putting on this summit event each year is a lot of work, but I so much look forward to putting it on and seeing my friends every year. They are my family, I sure hope it continues over the years. I'm not as capable of the effort these days. It is a little more difficult not living in Montreal. But I would still like to attend and enjoy time with these great friends for many more years.

CHAPTER
15
The Wonderful Years

You can't tell Andrée from the rest of the flowers.

For these wonderful years that I have known my very
best friend Andrée, I have never known her to miss a
Sunday going to church. She is a Catholic and sings in
the choir. I was a Protestant and I had not gone to church
except for Christmas and Easter in many years. I had
never attended a Catholic service before. But I decided to
go and hear Andrée sing in her choir. I started to go with
her most Sundays and I started to attend some church
and choir social events with her and met a very nice

group of people. A number of Sundays later a member of the Knights of Columbus gave a short message about their charity works in the community to the congregation, and he was wanting to recruit new members. I wanted to know a little more about this organization as I am now all about charity work and being an asset in helping others.

I sat down with this gentleman and liked what I heard about this men's Catholic group. I then took a Catechism course and joined the Catholic church.

There are four degrees of Knights and after joining the first degree it took me a few years to attain and graduate all four degrees of The Knights Of Columbus. Today I am a fourth degree Sir Knight and I hold a few executive positions. But mostly I have found a wonderful group of clean-living friends to socialize and work with on behalf of the community. I have the distinguished honour in being Worthy Sir Knight Of The Year.

We Knights built the Santa Claus parade float on my trailer for the last few years.

IAN COBB

Proud to serve my church, community and country.

We all do a lot of great charity work and we put on some fantastic dinners and different events in order to raise funds to help our different charities in our community. I enjoy being the Chef and we have super Knights that work together to make all of our events a success.

I am proud to be a very active member of the Knights of Columbus.

I have a personal message to people of all faiths, religions and followings around this world. Please remember, that no matter how many different names we might call Him, we all pray to the same God. We all need to learn how to understand, love, respect and celebrate all of our many differences and come together in peace and friendship. Do not let the bigots, racists and others divide us to control us; let us share of our many differences around this planet and not let difference divide us. God Bless.

My life has been greatly enriched by my charity work and finding great friends, especially Andrée. Indeed, recently I decided to buy what will probably be my last property, and I asked Andrée if she wanted to go in on it with me. It's a lovely waterfront condo, and I do hope we won't have to inhabit it anytime soon.

Andrée and my first and last waterfront property.
Whichever one of us dies last gets the window seat.

IAN COBB

Waterfront property at St. James Cemetery, Belleville overlooking the Bay of Quinte.

Writing this book is something I never thought I'd achieve. But now that I'm a writer, I will end with the gift of this little true story.

A TRUE CHRISTMAS STORY
— by Ian Cobb in 2018.

THE RETURN OF THE MAGIC SANTA CLAUS SLEIGH BELL.

We do not have any family dropping by the house this Christmas, so I will send this true Christmas story out to everyone!

It was Christmas eve at our ranch home in N.B. about 1982. Our three children were in pajamas and it was getting to be bedtime. When we heard a thump and a bump on the roof, and I immediately said "What was that ! Is he here already? you guys better get upstairs to bed or he will pass by, and the three of them flew up the stairs and jumped under the covers. Santa's note was on the kitchen table with his glass of milk and cookies. The bale of hay was put out in the front yard for Rudolf and his friends and the stockings were all in place.

Early in the morning three kids were on our bed telling us to get up that he had found our house alright and the stockings were full. So we all went downstairs and opened all our gifts. Then I spotted something outside on the circle driveway and we noticed that the hay was scattered all around the snow out front. There were hundreds of reindeer footprints all around in the snow. But there was still something on the driveway that we could not make out. So my oldest son Jeffrey put his coat and boots on, he was about eight years old, to fetch whatever it was. A few minutes later he came running into the house holding a very tarnished solid copper bell in his hand. I said that it must have been what we heard last night falling on our roof.

So we all agreed that it was from Santa's reindeer harness and we had to find a way to get it back to him, but how?. So we all decided to wait until next Christmas and leave a note with the bell for Santa!

This is exactly what we did. The note told Santa that we did not know his address at the North Pole, so we were returning his bell to him tonight. In the morning there was another note on the table from Santa saying that his elves had made another bell over the summer for his sleigh. He also said because you were very good and honest children in returning my magic bell, you could keep it and take good care of this magic bell and to hang on your tree every year. So this bell was hung up every Christmas since.

Even when we moved to Belleville, Ontario in 1993 we hung it with the wreath on our porch each year.

But around the year 2000 someone who came to our door decided that they needed this old looking bell and took it. That happened about eighteen years ago and we never saw it again.

Now it is Dec. 22nd, 2018 and Andrée and I are walking around downtown Belleville and we happened to walk into a second hand and antique shop at 52 Bridge St. E. We were only inside forty-five seconds when I spotted our magic bell standing on a table, priced for sale. Andree picked it up and before I touched it I went to the person at the cash and told her that they had my bell. I identified it by the bailing wire inside it holding a large nut from a bolt. And inside, at the top right hand corner there was a very slight crack in the corner where the seams come together; it had been hand made in the year 1890 and you could see the faintest light shining through this crack. Two days later I spoke to the owner at the store; Mike was his name. I told him I sure did not want to buy my own bell back from him, but I told him I had something to trade him for it, and I did. Tomorrow on Christmas day I am bringing the bell with me to show my grandchildren, and tell them the true story about "THE RETURN OF THE MAGIC SANTA CLAUS SLEIGH BELL."

The magic Santa Claus sleigh bell.

Me and my mom in the happiest of times.
Later, she would often find it difficult to know how to deal with me.

IAN COBB

ACKNOWLEDGEMENTS

A special thank you to my best friend Andrée Quinn who had the most patience and influence in helping me to read and write properly. Alayne Hing for her encouragement and help in writing my story, as well as everyone else who has supported me throughout my struggle in reproducing most of my life in my book.